MUSTANG
Selling the Legend

MUSTANG
Selling the Legend

Bob McClurg and Andy Willsheer

Motorbooks International
Publishers & Wholesalers ®

This edition first published in 1997 by
Motorbooks International Publishers & Wholesalers,
729 Prospect Avenue, PO Box 1, Osceola, WI 54020 USA

© Windrow & Greene 1997

Previously published by Windrow & Greene Ltd, London

Library of Congress Cataloging-in-Publication Data Available.

ISBN 0-7603-0317-7

Printed and bound in Spain

Front cover **At first glance, the 1967 Mustang seemed to be the same as the original model, but on closer inspection it could be seen to have a more aggressive appearance through revised front-end styling.**

Back cover **This "Sat. Nite Sizzle." ad appeared in 1981 and illustrates the Mustang Top Sport, a glamorized economy model that was styled to look like a convertible.**

Title page **In 1967, with other manufacturers chasing a piece of the ponycar market, Ford appealed to the loyalty of Mustang enthusiasts with a series of "Take the Mustang Pledge" ads.**

CONTENTS

INTRODUCTION

Virtually every successful advertising executive in history has lived, and died, by the credo, "It pays to advertise, and advertising pays!" Of course, it never hurts to be able to advertise a product that consumers will almost certainly purchase, and purchase in substantial quantities. That was exactly how the management of Ford Motor Company felt the day they unveiled their exciting new "personal car", the Ford Mustang, on April 17, 1964.

However, Ford also knew that they were charting previously unexplored territory. After all, their newly introduced Mustang broke with tradition by being America's first affordably priced, four-seat "personal car". In light of the rather large investment required to bring this new product to market, it was judicious that the American motoring public be made well aware of that fact.

In early 1962, representatives of Ford's long-standing advertising agency, J.Walter Thompson Inc, and JWT/Ford account executives Sid Olsen and Walter Murphy, were summoned to a summit meeting. Present were Ford's marketing director, Lee Iacocca, and Donald Frey, Hal Sperlich and Frank Zimmerman. On the agenda was the tentative marketing strategy for the yet-to-be-released (and named) Mustang, which Ford Division president Robert S. McNamara had scheduled for introduction in mid-1964.

Under consideration as the platform for this "personal car" were concept vehicles like the Allegro and Median, as well as Lee Iacocca's Falcon derived XT-Bird. In the end, the Falcon platform would serve as the car's base, although it would be cloaked with a wind cheating body that wouldn't resemble anything like the boxy Falcon.

But what would they call this exciting creation? During the ensuing months, a variety of names was proposed, including Cheetah, Puma, Thunderbird II, Cougar, Colt, Special Falcon, Torino and Mustang. Thankfully, Mustang prevailed. As history would later record, the name Mustang was considered as "American as hell" in the hallways of Ford's "Big Glass House" in Dearborn, Michigan.

It's possible that even Ford wasn't prepared for the overwhelming response generated by the Mustang's debut at the New York World's Fair. Almost overnight, the car became a favorite among patrons of the Walt Disney Magic Skyway attraction. However, that reaction paled in comparison to what was taking place at Ford dealers across the nation.

Fortunately, JWT advertising executives were well prepared, releasing a barrage of advertisement's, which appeared in magazines such as *Life*, *Look*, and *Time*. These proclaimed: "Mustang—exciting new car from Ford Motor Company...show stopper at the World's Fair!" Those initial advertisements were the precursors of hundreds more, all beautifully photographed and illustrated, that the world renowned advertising specialists would produce for Ford during the following 30 years.

In addition to examples of JWT's efforts, *Mustang: Selling the Legend* includes advertisements produced by other marketing companies for the special Mustangs, built by Carroll Shelby in the mid- to late sixties and, more recently, by Steve Saleen. It also celebrates and chronicles Americana in its purest state. Shown are oft-discarded, hard-to-find, advertising and promotional items enlisted in the sale of America's favorite ponycar: dealer promo models, hats, shirts, jackets, pins, key chains, lamps, cups, glasses and many other fascinating items.

Mustang: Selling the Legend is a celebration of the Mustang in all its forms, but from an informatively stimulating and decidedly different viewpoint. As a result, the authors and publishers hope that, like the automobile itself, it will become a treasured classic.

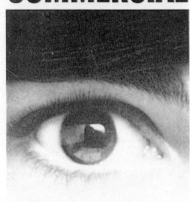

THE MOST EXCITING THING ON TV TONIGHT WILL BE A COMMERCIAL

GET YOUR FIRST GOOD LOOK AT THE YEAR'S MOST EXCITING NEW CAR...
...THE NEW FORD MUSTANG!
TONIGHT—9:30—ON:
HAZEL [NBC] · THE JIMMY DEAN
SHOW [ABC] · PERRY MASON [CBS]

1965

Right **From April 2 to April 30, 1964, Ford Division ran a series of advertisements, proclaiming: "The most exciting thing on TV tonight will be a commercial". And they were right! The prime-time television spots allowed viewers their first sight of the fantastic Mustang.**

CHAPTER 1

THE EARLY YEARS: 1964-66

When Ford Motor Company was ready to introduce the 1994 Mustang, an impressive gatefold poster appeared in the December 10, 1993 edition of *USA Today*, which best summed up America's — and the world's — 30-year love affair with this truly unique automobile by proclaiming: "It was was the horse that carried away a nation. Untamed spirit captured in chrome, it took the whole country for a spin. And we never came back."

The ride began on April 17, 1964, and what a ride it's been! Lithe in spirit, quick and agile like its namesake, and with an affordable base price of $2360^{00}, the Mustang was an immediate success. It would also prove to be as fearsome in motorsports competition as the fighter plane, which bore the same name, had been in the skies of war-torn Europe over 20 years before.

The Mustang was the brainchild of Ford president Robert S. McNamara, and it was in the personal charge of the young and aggressive Ford marketing director, Lido A. "Lee" Iacocca. However, of all the new cars produced by Ford Division in the last 40 years, the Mustang project, code name T-5, was more than just another car: it functioned as the springboard for the careers of many life-long Ford Motor Company employees, who came from all levels within the organization.

History, of course, records that the Mustang reached the marketplace after 18 short months of development, due in part to the incorporation of the subcompact Ford Falcon's 108in-wheelbase, multi-layered-sheetmetal, unibody platform. Initially, it was marketed in coupe and convertible forms, but a fastback was added shortly after.

The new car featured a front tread width of 56.0in on the V-8 model, and 55.4in for the six-cylinder version, with a standard rear tread width of 56.0in. Like the Falcon, the Mustang's front suspension consisted of independently suspended spindles, each incorporating a single lower control arm, working in concert with an upper A-arm. A 65mm anti-dive bar, Autolite hydraulic shock absorbers and coil springs completed the set-up, the six-cylinder models featuring softer springs than the heavier V-8s. Both manual and power-steering options were available.

Presenting the unexpected...
New Ford Mustang!

This is the car you never expected from Detroit. It is so distinctively beautiful it has received the Tiffany Award for Excellence in American Design, the first automobile ever to be so honored by Tiffany & Co. Mustang has the look, the fire, the flavor of one of the great European road cars. Yet it is as American as its name . . . and as practical as its price. Because Mustang is an amazingly versatile car and can be inexpensively tailored to the widest variety of individual tastes, many very different people will find it surprisingly easy to say: "This is the ideal car for me." Turn the page and you'll see why.

Left **"Presenting the unexpected...New Ford Mustang!" This was the very first of J.Walter Thompson's four-color magazine advertisements, which appeared in the likes of** *Life*, *Look*, *Time*, **etc, and heralded the release of the "distinctively beautiful" 1964½ Ford Mustang. It declared: "...the car you never expected from Detroit." Similarly, we doubt that Detroit — specifically Ford Division — ever expected to receive such a prestigious accolade as the Tiffany Award for Excellence in American Design, something that set a precedence in the automotive industry.**

This page **Ford conducted a national "Order Holding Program" through the newsprint medium, between April 2 and April 30, 1964. Since initially new cars were in short supply, this was a sure-fire way to guarantee potential buyers a brand-new Mustang whenever they were ready to purchase one. To qualify, all the prospective customer had to do was fill out a reservation form. In addition, he or she also received a personalized "Original Edition Mustang" nameplate. For an extra $2⁰⁰ dealer cost, one could also mail away for a 1/25-scale plastic model of a Mustang coupe (*below right*), made by AMT. This was available in Wimbledon White, Poppy Red or Caspian Blue, and it scored a genuine home run with non-licensed members of the family!**

UNEXPECTED LOOK

UNEXPECTED PRICE

designed to be designed by you

. . . and here's the equipment to design it with!

CONVENIENCE OPTIONS

- 260-cu. in. V-8
- 3-speed Cruise-O-Matic transmission
- Power steering
- Power brakes
- White sidewall tires
- Push-button radio

- Backup lights
- Deluxe seat belts front and rear
- Outside rearview mirror
- 2-speed electric wipers and washers
- Tinted windshield

LUXURY OPTIONS

- Full-length console between front seats
- Padded sun visors
- Rocker panel molding
- Deluxe wheel covers with simulated knock-off hubs

- Air conditioner
- Tinted glass
- Vinyl-covered hardtop roof
- Accent paint stripe
- Convertible with power-operated top and vinyl tonneau cover

PERFORMANCE OPTIONS

- 289-cu. in. V-8
- 4-speed manual transmission
- Heavy-duty battery

- Rally Pac (tachometer and clock)
- 14-inch wheels and tires

FORD MUSTANG

CDM 1254   LITHO IN U.S.A.

Out back, the Mustang's rear suspension utilized the Falcon 8in rear end, attached to a pair of three-leaf, semi-elliptic springs and Autolite hydraulic shocks. Rear end gearing varied from 2.80:1 down to 4.11:1, while braking was taken care of by dual servo/self adjusting, 9in, four-lug drum brakes on six-cylinder models, and 10in-diameter, five-lug drum brakes on the V-8 cars. If you purchased the mid-year Mustang GT option, you could enjoy the safety and convenience of 10½in front disc brakes as part of the package.

Rolling stock on this exciting new offering consisted of 13x4.5 and 14x5.0in, two-piece "safety rim" steel wheels, shod with 6.50x13 and 6.50x14in Kelly-Springfield bias-ply tyres. Six styles of hubcap were offered, including versions of the Fairlane wire wheel cap. Additionally, a 14x7in styled steel wheel and UniRoyal "Red Stripe" rubber would debut with the introduction of the Mustang GT.

The range of engine options for the Mustang began with the Falcon's humble 170cu.in, single-barrel carbureted inline-six, rated at 101hp. Leading the V-8 powertrain offerings was a 164hp,

260cu.in engine equipped with an Autolite two-barrel carburetor. Should Mustang owners desire more V-8 power — and who wouldn't? — they could opt for either the Autolite four-barrel equipped, 200hp 289, or the 210hp "Challenger" 289. By late June of that year, a 271hp 289 "K" engine would also be available as an option on special-order cars, and as standard with the GT package. There was a choice of three- or four-speed manual transmission, as well as a three-speed automatic.

Initially, the electrical system utilized the standard Ford 12-volt generator. However, towards the end of the year, this component was made obsolete by the introduction of the new Autolite 12-volt alternator.

So much for the steak. Now for the sizzle. The Mustang was offered in a multitude of hues, including Raven Black, Pagoda Green, Dynasty Blue, Caspian Blue, Rangoon Red, Silversmoke Gray, Wimbledon White, Prairie Bronze, Cascade Green, Sunlight Yellow, Vintage Burgundy, Skylight Blue, Chantilly Beige, Poppy Red, Twilight Turquoise and Phoenician Yellow.

While a great many Mustang enthusiasts assume that all early Mustangs came equipped with a pair of front bucket seats and a single rear bench seat, this was not always the case. Some early cars, especially six-cylinder models, came with a bucket-style front bench with a fold-down center armrest. Furthermore, one style of upholstery was used initially, which is now referred to as the standard vinyl interior. This featured seat and seat-back rolls with pleated inserts. There was a choice of three solid interior colors, five two-tone

Mustang—exciting new car from Ford Motor Company... show stopper at the World's Fair

Ford Motor Company is:

600 horses and a wild little pony

Husky ideas. Frisky ideas.
Our engineers keep trotting them out. From the brash little Mustang that nuzzled its way into America's heart, to a huge workhorse of a truck designed for tomorrow's superhighways. This super-hauler is our experimental 600 h.p.

Gas Turbine Truck. It will cruise at turnpike speeds and swallow up 600 miles between refuelings. The two-man cabin has TV, stove and refrigerator. It's a big hauler. In fact, only one thing carries more weight at Ford Motor Company—our insistence on top-notch quality in everything we build.

The bold engineering comes from... *Ford* MOTOR COMPANY

MUSTANG CHRONOLOGY – 1964

● Mustang is bestowed the Tiffany & Co. "Gold Medal Award for Excellence in Design", the first time it is ever bestowed upon an automobile.

● From April 2 to April 30, Ford Division runs a series of prime-time television spots, preceding them with magazine ads that announce: "The most exciting thing on TV tonight will be a commercial". They were right!

● To further gauge consumer response, the company places advertisements in newspapers across the country, debuting its "Order Holding Program". Part of that program includes a personalized "Original Edition Mustang" nameplate and, as further thanks, a 1/25-scale AMT plastic model — complete with data sheet — of America's soon-to-be favorite ponycar is appropriately offered in patriotic red, white or blue. The dealer cost is a mere $2^{00}, and the offer is made available to the first 50,000 buyers.

● A national hotel lobby display campaign is also run in conjunction with the Holiday Inn chain.

● As part of a PR blitz prior to the New York World's Fair, a 1964½ Mustang coupe is shown to an eager press corps on the observation platform of the Empire State building,

in downtown Manhattan. To accomplish this monumental feat, the car was dismantled and carried, piece by piece, in the freight elevator to the top of the building, where it was subsequently re-assembled!

● The Mustang becomes a favorite with the crowds attending the World's Fair in Flushing Meadows, where it receives extensive exposure — along with other Ford products — on the Walt Disney Magic Skyway, or Ford's Roads To The World, as the attraction was also called.

● The Mustang is selected as the official pace car of the Indianapolis 500 on May 31. A total of 37 Wimbledon White D-code Indy 500 Pace Car convertibles, with blue GT stripes, are prepared. Among this sizeable group are four K-code Hi-Po 289 cars, which are used for the actual parade lap activities. Benson Ford is the honorary Grand Marshall. Also part of that program is the Green and Checkered Flag Contest, in which the 105 top Ford new car salesmen from across the US are awarded similarly adorned Indianapolis 500 Mustang Pace Car coupe replicas. In addition, 105 matching AMT Midget Mustang pedal cars and 1/25-scale AMT Pace Car coupe models are awarded to the salesmen for their sterling efforts.

● 100,000 new Mustangs are sold within the first 90 days.

● The Mustang makes its screen debut in the James Bond movie *Goldfinger*, in which agent 007 and his Aston Martin effectively disable a Springtime Yellow convertible, driven by Tilley Masterson, after a memorable chase.

● The Mustang 2+2 fastback debuts as a companion to the already fast selling coupe and convertible in September 1964.

● The stamped-metal AMF Midget Mustang and the Cox manufactured, 1/12-scale, battery powered, plastic-bodied Mustang coupe are made available to future Ford buyers through a special Christmas season magazine and dealer sales promotion. The price of these novelties is a whopping $12^{95} each!

● *Playboy* magazine's Playmate of the Year, Donna Michelle, is awarded a specially painted Playboy Pink 1964½ Mustang convertible as part of the "booty" given annually to the publication's top model.

● By the end of 1964, Mustang mania has thoroughly consumed America, with a total of 160,000 examples of the new ponycar sold!

Left **World's Fair promotion aside, perhaps the most aggressive new-car publicity campaign of 1964 occurred over the Memorial Day Weekend, during the Indianapolis 500 at the famed "Brickyard". The new Mustang or, to be precise, 37 new Mustangs paced the historic motorsports event and were used throughout the month-long Indy 500 festivities.**

Left and far left **Part of the same campaign was the Green and Checkered Flag Contest, in which the top salesmen from Ford dealers across the country were awarded Indianapolis 500 Mustang Pace Car coupe replicas, AMF Midget Mustang pedal cars and AMT 1/25-scale Pace Car coupe models. One of the few surviving examples of the coupe is shown here, along with a pristine AMT Pace Car model.**

13

Now–just in time for Christmas– only at your Ford Dealer's!

MIDGET MUSTANG

Specially priced at only

$12⁹⁵

While they last!

Here's a child's gift that'll look just as inviting under a Christmas tree as a 1965 Mustang will look in your driveway. The solid, all-metal Midget Mustang, that you might expect to see offered for $25.00, has easy-to-use pedals, make-believe shift lever and real rubber tires. Give your child a Midget Mustang this Christmas–for a taste of the fun all Mustangers enjoy! Stop in at your participating Ford Dealer's and pick one up for only $12.95, suggested list price . . . at no obligation. For $2.00 more, dealer can order for delivery to your doorstep.

Best year yet to go Ford

MUSTANG! MUSTANG! MUSTANG!

A PRODUCT OF Ford MOTOR COMPANY

Gift idea for the whole family! 1965 Mustang– the most successful new car ever introduced in America!

These pages **In their continuing effort to publicize the new Mustang, Ford dealers offered these exciting Mustang miniatures, fittingly "just in time for Christmas!" Shown is the AMF Midget Mustang pedal car** (*right and facing page, left*), **which sold for a whopping $12⁹⁵ (or $15⁰⁰ fully assembled), and a battery powered, 1/12-scale plastic Mustang coupe** (*facing page, right*). **The latter cost a mere $4⁹⁵. Today, pristine examples of these toys are worth much more.**

designs, and a varied assortment o vinyl and cloth combinations.

As could be expected, interior appoint ments and options were numerous ranging from the basic instrumenta tion/AM radio/standard upholstery all th way up to the Decor Option Group, intro duced in March 1965. This included th distinctive "running-horse" seat inser upholstery, bolstered seats and doc panels, padded sun visors, woodgrai appliques, five-dial gauge cluster, a ful length console, and combination Rally Pac clock/tachometer.

Upon the introduction of the Mustan GT, in late 1965, ponycar purchaser could also personalize their new toy with exterior appointments like trumpe exhaust extensions that passed throug the lower rear valance, European-styl fog lamps, and GT side stripes and fend er badges.

Oh, and one other thing. In early 1965 a guy by the name of Carroll Shelb entered the picture with the introductio of 36 specially prepared, 2+2 R-mode Mustangs, which had been born 'n' bre for out-and-out racing. These lightweig GT-350s, as they were known, capture the 1965 SCCA B/Production title. The were soon followed by the limited-pro duction street-version: the Shelb GT-350 Mustang. The rest, as the say, was history.

Freshened up for '66

Although the 1966 ponycar was almost mirror image of its predecessors, numer ous styling and engineering change had been made to keep the car "fresh and encourage sales, not that Ford ha any difficulty in selling the proverbia

MUSTANG CHRONOLOGY – 1965

● Working in conjunction with racing great Carroll Shelby, Ford prepares 36 lightweight, Mustang R-model Shelby GT-350 fastbacks in September, as part of a factory sponsored assault on the Corvette dominated SCCA B/Production road racing class.

● In similar fashion, six Holman & Moody prepared, 427 SOHC Mustang fastbacks and six tunnel-port, 427 wedge powered A/FX fastbacks are prepared to do battle in NHRA's highly contested A/FX factory experimental class. Tasca Ford's Bill Lawton sweeps the eliminator at both the AHRA and NHRA Winternationals professional drag races.

● One year after the Mustang's introduction, Ford Division's product planning manager, Donald Frey, and president, Lee Iacocca, pose with Mustang #417,000, as designated by the special "417 X 417" license plate (417,000 cars sold by April 17). In reality, however, the sales figure for the ponycar was closer to 418,000 units by that date.

● The Mustang GT option debuts in mid-April.

● In November, Hertz Rent-A-Car Corporation enters into a contract with Shelby American to purchase 200 black-and-gold Shelby GT-350 Mustangs to add to the company's rental fleet. In December, the number is increased to 1000 specially prepared Shelby GT-350H Mustangs. So begins the Hertz "Rent-A-Racer" legend.

● Shelby American team drivers, led by *Sports Car Graphic* magazine's editor, Jerry Titus, wrest the SCCA B/Production class title from Chevrolet's Corvette.

Right and facing page, left
With the advent of the GT option in mid-April 1965, Ford Division and JWT not only pushed the package (with ads like the one shown), but they also touted the benefits of dolling-up that plain looking ponycar by employing a wide array of GT inspired, bolt-on accessories. These were readily available through Ford dealers.

"wads" out of this already refreshingly unique car. By the end of 1965, the company had already sold a total of 680,989 Mustangs.

Style-wise, the most notable exterior changes included an extruded aluminum, multi-bar front grille in place of the stamped honeycomb version previously used. Extruded aluminum rocker panel mouldings and back-up lights, which had been options on the early models, were now standard equipment. Furthermore, the sculpted "scoop" area aft of the door featured a three-bar, chrome-plated trim piece, installed on every model except the GT. The newest ponycar's rear mounted gas cap had also been significantly restyled, as had its side mirrors, upscale models having a remote-control, cable operated mirror on the driver's side. Of course, wheel decor — both hubcaps and styled steel wheels

Give your car a GT flair!
Your Ford Dealer has the goods

— received upgrades, too. Finally, on Mustang GTs and K-option cars, there was a twin-flag, aluminum front fender badge that proudly proclaimed: "289 High Performance".

Inside, perhaps the biggest news was that the Mustang had successfully broken away from the commonplace "idiot light" instrumentation with the introduction of a five-dial, half-swept instrument panel, complete with walnut applique and 140mph speedometer. The last had originally been an option on the GT and had also been included as part of the Interior Decor Option, but now it was standard across the board. The optional Faria manufactured clock and tachometer module had been totally restyled, but it was still offered in six- and eight-grand versions.

The density of the foam filled dashpad had been increased for safety reasons. Newly introduced that year was breathable vinyl seat upholstery, later termed as "Comfortweave". The Mustang's Interior Decor Group option door panels were also restyled to include a built-in, foam filled armrest, integrating the restyled door handle and handle cup directly into the panel. Combination red and white door panel courtesy lights became standard on upscale models, along with the highly acclaimed "day & nite" rear-view mirror and deluxe edition seat belts. An AM/FM/8-track cartridge/radio was offered for the first time, as was the highly sought after, simulated woodgrain (read that "plastic") GT steering wheel.

Underneath the 1966 Mustang's hood, the 120hp, 200cu.in, inline six-cylinder engine still functioned as the ponycar's most basic powerplant. Next came the

If they're still waiting for Agnes down at the Willow Lane Whist and Discussion Group, they'll wait a long time. Agnes hasn't been herself since she got her Mustang hardtop (with its racy lines, bucket seats, smooth, optional 3-speed automatic transmission and fire-eating 200 cu. in. Six). Mustang is more car than Willow Lane has seen since the last Stutz Bearcat bit the dust. (And Agnes has a whole new set of hobbies, none of which involves cards.) Why don't you find out if there's any truth in the rumor–Mustangers have more fun?

Best year yet to go Ford
**MUSTANG!
MUSTANG!
MUSTANG!**

200hp, 2-V 289cu.in V-8, followed by a series of tuned small-block V-8's, ranging from the 225hp Challenger, through the 271hp K-engine option, to the Shelby tweaked, 306hp, "Cobra-ized" 289. Various carburetor and high-performance exhaust options were made available that year, via both Ford Parts and Services and Shelby American. Backing up these powerplants was everything from a standard floor-mount,

Above **Classic Mustang advertising almost always appealed to the adventurous side in all of us. This ad is typical. It refers to "Agnes" and her transformation from dull to dashing, which began the day she purchased a 200cu.in, six-cylinder 1965 Mustang coupe. Well, if not entirely factual, at least it's an imaginative story.**

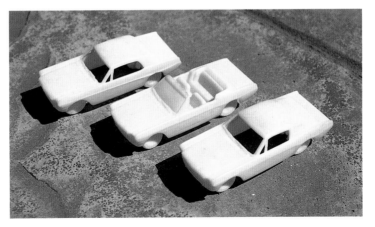

This page **With the Mustang's rapidly escalating popularity, toy and novelty manufacturers quickly jumped on the ponycar bandwagon. Lesney, maker of the popular British Matchbox Series toy line, introduced this steerable, 1/64-scale, diecast model of the Mustang 2+2 (*top left*). On the other hand, all one had to do was consume a box of Shredded Wheat breakfast cereal to retrieve any one of these three 1/64-scale, injection molded Mustang toys (*top right*). The trio of "tintype" Mustangs are European in origin and highly collectible (*left*).**

Facing page **This pristine example of a Mustang bed spread is guaranteed to make the mini-Mustanger crawl sleepily beneath the covers to take an imaginary late-night cruise.**

Right In the early days, Ford never missed an opportunity to capitalize on the Mustang's attributes, as clearly demonstrated by this 1/25-scale Philco-Ford Mustang 2+2 transistor radio. The speaker grille is inside the car, while the controls are on the underside.

Right This 1/25-scale Tomy Toys Super Power Gas Station is one of the many toys that were based on Ford's popular ponycar.

three-speed manual transmission to a C-4 three-speed automatic.

Suspension, brake and wheel/tire packages remained virtually the same. The exceptions to this rule, however, were the K-model and Shelby GT-350, both of which received a heavier-duty 9in Traction-Lok rear end.

Aside from the Mustang GT, the Shelby GT-350 continued to be top dog in competition, establishing itself by firmly defeating all comers and, in the process, winning the 1965 SCCA B/Production Championship. The year-old Shelby Mustang also had a counterpart, of sorts, with the release of 1000 specially equipped, black-and-gold Shelby GT-350H Mustangs, which were available for rental only through the Hertz Rent-A-Car network. The "H" suffix in the car's title stood for "Hertz".

Coincidentally, Ford's Rocky Mountain (Colorado) Region dealers introduced

their own idea of what a special-edition Mustang should look like. Appropriately, this was christened the High Country Special, or HCS, as these cars have become known. Aside from sporting a small "High Country Special" badge on each fender flank, directly above the running-horse emblem, these cars were available in three special colors that depicted the Rocky Mountain territory: Aspen Gold, Columbine Blue and Timberline Green.

Ford also got in on this act by offering a Limited Edition Mustang Hardtop and a Sprint 200 special-edition hardtop to celebrate the sale of over one million Mustangs. These coupes were powered by the baseline six-cylinder engine and were distinguished by personalized plaques in their Decor Group optioned interiors. The Sprint 200 also had a custom decal on the air cleaner.

Left **"If it ain't broke, don't fix it," a phrase that could easily sum up both Ford's and J.Walter Thompson's approach to the Mustang's runaway sales success. After all, when you're selling everything you can make, why change the advertising strategy, a point made by this 1966 *Look* magazine advertisement.**

21

This page **Prior to Ford Division assuming control of the Shelby Mustang program in mid-1967, Shelby American's designer/art director, Peter Brock (of Shelby Cobra Daytona Coupe fame), and artist George Bartell handled most of that company's advertising. As you can see, the ads are racer oriented and devoid of the hyperbole that typified Ford's corporate ads. However, we have a faint suspicion that the Hertz advertisement shown was (corporate) advertising agency inspired.**

MUSTANG CHRONOLOGY – 1966

● Thermactor exhaust system introduced on all V-8 equipped cars to comply with California's newly instituted anti-pollution laws.

● Three-speed C-4 automatic transmission offered for first time with 271hp K-code equipped cars.

● Facing a shortage of 289 V-8 engines, Ford and J.Walter Thompson executives devise the six-cylinder Sprint 200 to celebrate the sale of the millionth Mustang in March.

● Shelby's GT-350 becomes "soft" with the inclusion of a fold-down rear seat and optional C-4 automatic transmission. The performance Mustang also receives Plexiglass side windows and a choice of two custom wheel styles (cast aluminum Shelby ten-spoke or chrome-plated Magnum 500 sculpted steel). It is also available in colors other than traditional white.

● Faced with stiff competition in the A/FX-cum-"Match Racer" class, the Ford drag team unveils six stretched-wheelbase, tubular-framed, fiberglass-bodied Mustang fastbacks, built by Holman & Moody. They are powered by fuel injected, nitromethane burning versions of the 427 SOHC engine.

● Three plants — Dearborn in Michigan, Metuchen in New Jersey and San Jose in California — are all busily churning out Mustangs to meet the overwhelming demand.

● Due to copyright laws in Germany, the name "Mustang" cannot be applied to cars sold to GIs through military bases. The original project code, T-5, is adopted instead.

● For the second consecutive year, a Shelby GT-350 Mustang, piloted by Jerry Titus, wins the SCCA B/Production class title — now renamed "Trans-Am".

You'd love to answer the call of Mustang? Good! There are three new ways: hardtop, fastback and convertible! Standard for '67? Bucket seats, carpeting, floor shift, Ford Motor Company Lifeguard-Design safety features, more. Now what? Options that say you!

Stereo Tape, handling package, SelectShift automatic transmission that also works manually, V-8's up to 390-cu.-in., power front disc brakes, bench seat, tilt-away steering wheel, AM-FM radio, air conditioning. Smitten? Great! May we pronounce you "Man and Mustang?"

'67 MUSTANG
Bred first...to be first

Right **As a precautionary measure, particularly in light of the influx of non-Ford entries into ponycar territory, in 1967 Ford Division and JWT embarked upon a series of magazine advertisements that appealed to Mustang loyalists to "answer the call to Mustang". With year-end ponycar sales reaching an all-time high, legions of loyal Mustangers must have responded to that call!**

RE-ESTABLISHING THE HOME TURF: 1967-68

As 1967 dawned, having enjoyed two-and-a-half years of uncontested leadership in the personal car market, which the Mustang had essentially created, America's premier pony-car was beginning to be pressured by a series of interlopers. These ponycar "wanna-bes" came from the likes of General Motors, Chrysler Corporation and, yes, even American Motors! Realizing that you're only an automotive industry leader if you continue to lead, Ford debuted the restyled 1967 Mustang at a time when the competition was beginning to revel in the (short lived) glory of having finally produced personal car packages of their own!

The Mustang for 1967 was slightly larger, being wider by 2.7in and taller by ½in. Aesthetically, the car still resembled its predecessor, but it featured a more aggressive body profile with a significantly larger grille opening. Ford's new ponycar was also given a totally restyled concave rear panel, with a trio of curved, vertical taillight lenses at each end, which provided superior night visibility. Exterior Decor Group options were offered that year and included such items as a functional twin-reverse-scooped hood (with rear facing turn signals), a special extruded aluminum ribbed taillight panel and a pop-open gas cap. The traditional concave body side panel had also been increased in size, giving the new model an even bolder appearance. In all, 20 exterior colors were available for the new car.

While the 1967 Mustang had been dramatically restyled on the outside, its exterior dimensions had also been expanded to accommodate some significant engineering upgrades. Let's start with the powertrains. Aside from the tried 'n' true, 200cu.in straight-six, one could choose from no less than four separate versions of the 289 small-block V-8: the C-code 200hp 2-V model; the A-code 225hp, Autolite 4-V equipped unit; the high-performance, K-code, 271hp, Holley 4-V equipped version; and the 306hp Shelby GT-350 package.

For the first time, a new 390cu.in, 320hp, Thunderbird Special FE-series big-block powerplant was made available in the Mustang GT and GTA (the letter "A" indicated that an automatic transmission was fitted). And, if that wasn't enough, Ford also shoehorned a

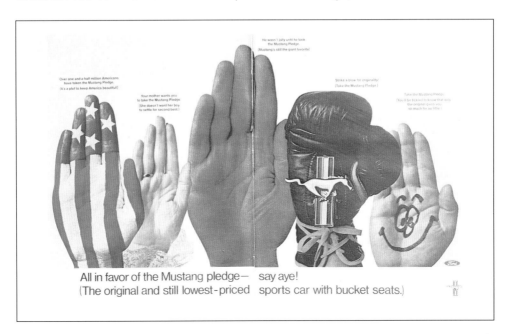

All in favor of the Mustang pledge— say aye! (The original and still lowest-priced sports car with bucket seats.)

Left **Ford devised another clever ad campaign that also traded on brand loyalty. These ads urged buyers to "take the Mustang pledge", and cited the fact that during the previous three years, over 1.5 million Mustang loving Americans had done precisely that.**

Right
Occasionally bordering on the comical, Ford's "Mustang pledge" ads may seem silly in retrospect. At the time, however, they were seen as being in tune with the carefree lifestyle that a great many youthfully-minded Americans embraced throughout the sixties.

Far right **Having invested heavily in the Shelby Mustang program, Ford Division was intent on exploiting the Shelby connection to the full, as illustrated by this ad. It succinctly emphasizes the finer points of owning a Mustang GT or GTA, or Shelby GT-350 or GT-500.**

55hp, 428cu.in Police Interceptor V-8 engine package into the new ponycar. This was specifically targeted at the Shelby line, although in some rare instances, it was not restricted solely to those models.

Backing it all up was an assortment of transmissions, beginning with the lowly three-speed manual and small-block Borg-Warner T-10 four-speed. The king of the "sticks", of course, was the famed top loader four-speed, normally found in the 390 and 428 cars. Then there was the most commonly employed three-speed C-4 automatic and, finally, an optional SelectShift heavy-duty C-6 automatic.

The new Mustang's dual-control-arm/coil-spring front suspension featured strategically relocated suspension pickup points, employing a pair of manual cam adjusters for setting camber and castor. This setup also employed larger ½in-diameter rubber suspension bushings, along with a substantially stronger lower control arm. On big-block cars, the spring rates were uprated to handle the extra load. Autolite shocks remained the norm. Another front-end improvement was quicker-ratio steering. This new model was also the first to incorporate a dual hydraulic braking system; 1in-larger-diameter front rotors were standard on all disc brake equipped cars.

At the rear, the Mustang retained its parallel twin-leaf-spring suspension, although this had been beefed up to compensate for the new vehicle's larger size. Two rear axle configurations were available, an 8 or 9in differential being employed depending on the powertrain application. Gear ratios varied from a 2.83:1, on the baseline car, down to

Left "**Carroll Shelby Presents <u>The</u> Road Cars....GT-350 and GT-500 For 1967**". And old Shel really meant it! For the first time in the Shelby Mustang's three-year production run, the car truly possessed an identity of its own. Compared to the fairly aggressively restyled 1967 Mustang, the new Shelby's trim coachwork made it look like a buckboard!

Below **Red Rocker and Van Halen lead singer, Sammy "I can't drive 55" Hagar with his 427 powered 1967 GT-500.**

Right **This particular advertisement promoted both sides of the Mustang: practicality and sportiness. Of course, the most obvious solution would be a two-car Mustang family. Wouldn't any Ford dealer just love that?**

Below **The 1967 Mustang had slightly more aggressive styling than its predecessor.**

3.25:1 on the GTA. Also new for 1967 were 14x6in slotted steel styled wheels, normally with Firestone F-70x14in Wide Oval rubber.

Inside, an optional Tilt-Away steering column and padded safety-hub steering wheel were big news. Gone was the central speedometer surrounded by four gauges: the new Mustang's instrument panel took on a space-age appearance, featuring a large speedometer and optional 6000rpm tachometer, mounted side by side. Gasoline, oil and amps gauges were offset.

The optional running-horse upholstery was also no longer available. However, comfort was improved with wider seats and thicker foam padding in myriad color combinations of breathable vinyl and cloth. The previously optional "day 'n' nite" rear-view mirror was now a standard fitting, while a full-length console with radio could be ordered, along with a four-light convenience control panel. The Deluxe interior option door panel boasted a moulded armrest, somewhat similar to the earlier model. Other optional amenities, such as air conditioning, a remote-control side mirror and an AM/FM/8-track stereo radio/tape player were all welcome creature comforts in the new ponycar.

Compared to the Shelby GT-350 and GT-500 models, however, the 1967 Mustang had received a mere facelift. The muscular Shelbys were in a league of their own, readily distinguishable from their more mundane counterparts. They boasted radically styled, fiberglass "fish-mouth" front panels and spoiler-decked rear quarters, complete with a battery of taillights borrowed from the Thunderbird. Their flanks featured a pair of functiona air intakes, which diverted air to both the passenger compartment and the rear brakes to prevent any overheating under severe usage.

Both cars had a fiberglass hood, which was held in place by a pair of locking pins and had an aggressive looking, dual-air-inlet scoop. Dual exhaust systems terminated in a quartet of tailpipes — two per side — which emerged from the sculpted rear valance. Three different wheel options were available that year: a 15in steel safety rim with mag-style hubcap, a 15in Kelsey-Hayes five-spoke styled steel wheel, and a 15in version of the previous year's distinctive ten-spoke aluminum wheel. All came wrapped in F-70x15in Goodyear Polyglas tires.

With seven vivid colors to choose from, the 1967 Shelby Mustang was strikingly handsome. But the Shelbys' main attributes were based on performance, not good looks. Three engine options were available, one being quite rare. The GT-350's 306hp, "Cobra-ized" 289 small-block featured an aluminum high-rise intake manifold, fitted with a 715cfm Holley 4-V carburetor for stickshift cars, or a 595cfm Autolite 4-V carburetor for automatic models. Ford Hi-Po cast-iron exhaust manifolds, an Autolite dual-point distributor, special "Cobra Powered by Ford" finned aluminum valve covers, and a chrome-plated air cleaner containing a paper element distinguished this particular model from the rest.

The GT-500's 335hp, 390cu.in FE-series big-block featured a dual-quad Cobra aluminum intake manifold and a pair of 600cfm in-line Holleys as standard. Other normal equipment included

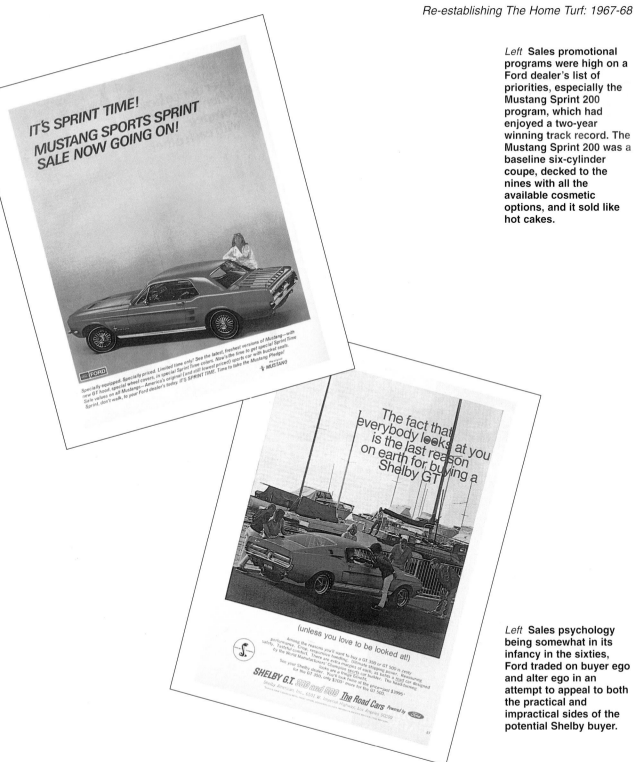

Left **Sales promotional programs were high on a Ford dealer's list of priorities, especially the Mustang Sprint 200 program, which had enjoyed a two-year winning track record. The Mustang Sprint 200 was a baseline six-cylinder coupe, decked to the nines with all the available cosmetic options, and it sold like hot cakes.**

Left **Sales psychology being somewhat in its infancy in the sixties, Ford traded on buyer ego and alter ego in an attempt to appeal to both the practical and impractical sides of the potential Shelby buyer.**

29

an Autolite dual-point distributor, Ford Hi-Po cast-iron headers, special "Cobra Le Mans" finned aluminum valve covers and a distinctive finned aluminum oval air cleaner.

For a very brief period, Shelby also offered a 427cu.in side-oiler version of the GT-500, presumably to use up the remaining inventory of engines from the discontinued 427SC Cobra project. However, this model was phased out early in the production year. Although no factual production data exists for these

cars, it has been estimated that approximately 50 were produced.

THE HITS KEEP ON COMING!

Physically, the differences between the 1967 Mustang and the 1968 model were minor. To go along with the "keep things fresh" attitude that appeared to rule the auto industry in those days, discernible, though subtle, cosmetic upgrades were made. For a more streamlined appearance, Ford did away with the traditional

"FORD" chromed block letters on the Mustang's hood, along with the free-standing pony "corral" in the grille cavity. The latter was reduced to a uni-dimensional piece of chrome trim, affixed to the grille.

Side marker reflectors were all the rage in 1968, and the Mustang sported a prominent set. One was located on the lower quarter of each front fender, while another was placed aft of each rear quarter panel, directly in line with the top of the rear bumper.

These pages **Throughout the Mustang's 30-year history, toys and other promotional items have played an important role in dealer/customer relations. The reasoning behind this was that if you grew up playing with a miniature version of a Ford product, you might be more inclined to buy the real thing at a later date. In the winter of 1967, Ford dealers offered a 1/12-scale, battery-powered AMF Mustang fastback "just In time for Christmas"** (*facing page, top*). **Or, if you were fortunate, a Ford salesman might have awarded your mom or dad a 1/25-scale, Philco/Ford 1967 Mustang transistor radio** (*facing page, bottom*). **Then, if you talked real nice to the man in the Ford service department, you could probably snap up one of the AMT 1/25-scale dealer promo Mustangs for a nominal fee. However, if you struck out on all fronts, you could always pedal on down to the local "five and dime", and purchase a Japanese Mustang tin model** (*right*).

MUSTANG CHRONOLOGY — 1967

● Numerous sales slogans and promotional programs are adopted for the Mustang to test brand loyalty and promote the new models. Among these are: "Bred to be first!...Mustang '67", "Take the Mustang pledge!" and "How do you improve on a classic?"

● Carroll Shelby and championship driver Jerry Titus enter a specially prepared 1967 Mustang coupe in SCCA Trans-Am competition, sporting black and yellow Terlingua Racing Team colors. The team fights tooth and nail with the Penske/Donahue-Sonoco/Camaro factory team in a fender bending melee to take the championship for a second consecutive season.

● The new 390 Mustang GT and GTA models are hot copy. Many top automotive magazines, such as *Hot Rod*, *Car Craft*, *Super Stock & Drag Illustrated*, *Motor Trend* and *Car & Driver*, test the new Mustang's mettle. Not surprisingly, Ford's ponycar earns high marks.

● For a second time, Ford dealers offer a 1/12-scale, motorized plastic Mustang through a special promotion timed to coincide with Christmas. The list price is $12.95.

● Ford dealers hold special sales promotions in an attempt to downplay the Chevrolet Camaro's auspicious debut.

● In honor of the Indianapolis 500, a Pacesetter Special Mustang hardtop, featuring racy body side stripes, is marketed throughout the Midwest.

● Special-edition Mustangs begin popping up everywhere. Dallas, Texas, Ford dealers devise the Blue Bonnet Special. Rocky Mountain Region dealers maintain a good thing with a 1967 rendition of the popular High Country Special. Twister Mustangs appear in Kansas, while in Canada, Toronto Ford dealers offer their own version of the Mustang Sprint, named the Third Birthday Treat. Down in Mexico, Carroll Shelby and Eduardo Velasquez enter into an agreement to produce Shelby de Mexico GT-350s, based on the locally produced Mustang coupe.

● Racing great Mario Andretti sets a series of land speed records at the Bonneville Salt Flats, driving Autolite-1, a DOHC, Ford Indianapolis-engined Mustang fastback. Recording speeds of well over 200mph, the car earns the title "World's fastest Mustang".

● The lease on Shelby's Los Angeles Airport facility expires. New car production is assumed by A.O. Smith Company in Livonia, Michigan.

31

Right and facing page, left
Only Mustang makes it happen, and makes it happen with class! Again, these advertisements play on the Walter Mitty fantasy. In one, mild-mannered "Sidney" has his life changed by a Candy-apple red, white-striped Mustang GT. Lucky Sidney! The other ad shows virtually the same transformation, only with a member of the opposite sex. Sorry, we didn't get the heroine's name.

Right and facing page, right
As exciting as the 1968 Mustangs may have been, the real news for Mustang performance enthusiasts happened out on the starting line of the NHRA Winternationals at Pomona Raceway in California. There, a fleet of ten Bill Stroppe prepared, white, SS/F and SS/FA 428 Cobra Jet powered Mustang fastbacks thoroughly trounced the competition in Super Stock Eliminator. Ford proudly ran an ad, proclaiming: "Hot Rod Sees the Light". Also shown is Hubert "Hube Baby" Platt and his SS/EA Cobra Jet Mustang, in action at the famed Orange County International Raceway in Southern California.

Still available that year, on V-8 models only, was the Mustang GT Equipment Group. This comprised low-restriction dual exhaust tips, a pop-up gas cap, GT emblems, reflective "C" side stripes, a pair of 4in, grille mounted fog/driving lights, GT styled steel wheels (either painted argent or chrome plated), F70x14in Firestone Wide Oval tires, heavy-duty suspension and a chrome engine dress-up kit. The optional factory louvered hood could also be ordered in semi-gloss black to contrast with the standard body color.

Creature comforts remained virtually the same, with the exception of the much maligned safety-pad steering wheel. The popular Tilt-Away steering column was retained, however.

That year, the ever popular Interior Decor Group option was part of the package. It consisted of simulated wood-grain appliques almost everywhere you looked, accompanied by two-tone door panels, which featured spring-loaded, flip-open handles and integral armrest pads. Interior trim was similarly updated and included the now infamous, clothes snagging rectangular metal buttons on the seatbacks. An overhead console, complete with its own map lights, was also offered, along with an optional electric clock, SelectAire air conditioning and three different styles of Philco/Ford push-button radio.

By mid-year, the ubiquitous 289cu.in small-block V-8 had been phased out of production. In its place, Ford substituted a slightly enlarged version of the same engine, displacing 302cu.in and available in both 2-V and 4-V forms. The latter pumped out 230hp, a mere 5hp more than its predecessor, but it was equa

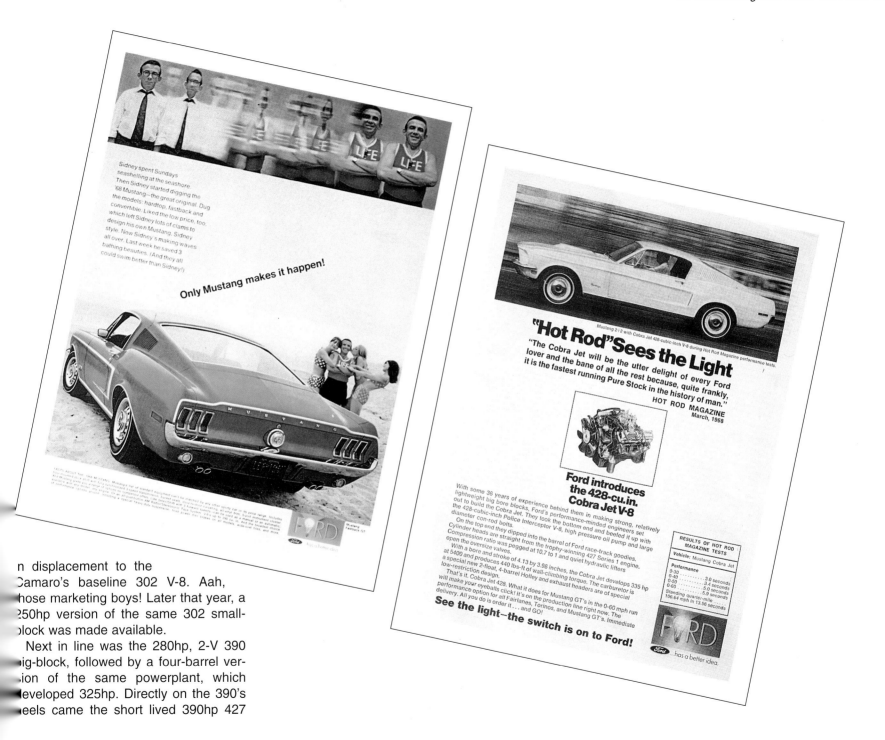

RESULTS OF HOT ROD MAGAZINE TESTS	
Vehicle: Mustang Cobra Jet	
Performance	
0-30	3.0 seconds
0-40	3.4 seconds
0-50	5.0 seconds
0-60	5.9 seconds
Standing quarter-mile	106.64 mph in 13.56 seconds

n displacement to the Camaro's baseline 302 V-8. Aah, hose marketing boys! Later that year, a 250hp version of the same 302 small-block was made available.

Next in line was the 280hp, 2-V 390 big-block, followed by a four-barrel version of the same powerplant, which developed 325hp. Directly on the 390's heels came the short lived 390hp 427

FE engine and a pair of 428s, one of which was a low-compression version that produced a mere 335hp. The other was the notorious 360hp 428 Cobra Jet, or CJ, as it was affectionately nicknamed. Of course, there was also the baseline straight-six, which was available that year in two sizes: 200cu.in (discontinued mid-year) and its replacement, the 250cu.in version.

Transmission choices remained virtu- ally the same as before, but rear ends varied. They ranged from a limited-slip, 2.79:1, 8in live axle to a 9in Traction Lok with 3.50:1 gear ratio.

By mid-year, a special Shelby GT-500, known as the KR (King of the Road), became available. This sported a 335hp Ram Air 428 Cobra Jet engine. Although not production models, perhaps the biggest news of 1968 was the release of 50 white, Bill Stroppe prepared, 428 Cobra Jet Mustang fastbacks, which were slated for competition in the National Hot Rod Association's Super Stock Eliminator category. On the cars' first outing, Ford racer Al Joniac took top honors, and all the bucks, establishing a tradition that was to continue for many years to come.

While cosmetic upgrades were kept to a bare minimum on the mainstream Mustang, the low-production Shelby

2 new low-priced Mustang Sprints on sale.

Save now on the two newest reasons why Mustang, the Original, is America's all-time sporty success car. New Mustang Sprints are specially equipped with GT stripes, pop-open gas cap, wheel covers, and special trim…at a special low price.

And when you choose a V-8 you also save on wide oval tires, styled steel wheels, GT fog lamps, plus all the standard features that keep all Mustangs ahead of the pack.

See the new Mustang Sprints today. Find out why the switch is on to Ford!

FORD'S SEE-THE-LIGHT SALE

Right **With the introduction of the new Mustang, account executives at J.Walter Thompson devised a "See the Light" campaign. In this instance, Ford's "See-the-Light Sale" makes the Mustang Sprint the center of attention.**

appeared to function as a rolling testbed for advanced styling ideas. For example, the 1968 grille opening was much larger in size, comically resembling a big-mouthed bass, complete with embedded fish hook — actually the bumper! Inside the grille cavity, one could find a set of grille mounted Lucas fog lamps. From the side, both 1967 and 1968 cars looked similar. The same could also be said of the back end. Or could it?

Back again was the 1967 Shelby's wall-to-wall taillight panel, which had been pirated from the Ford Thunderbird. Like the T'bird, the Shelby utilized the sequential taillight feature, an item that would soon become established as a Shelby trademark.

New to the line was a convertible that was equipped with a foam padded Sport Bar. This had sliding retaining rings for, of all things, surfboards!

Above and left **The ad reads: "Only Mustang and Carroll Shelby could make this happen!", and that's about right. Lee Iacocca had made the right choice. Although Shelby himself was no longer active in car manufacturing, he continued to function as a spokesman and media figure on behalf of the latest ponycars that bore his name.**

Above The phrasing may have been changed slightly from the previous ad, but the message is the same. This particular ad shows several versions of the 1968 Shelby at play and, well, more play! It also makes reference to the ultra-rare, short lived 427 engine option.

Above right An example of the ultimate Shelby: the GT-500KR.

MUSTANG CHRONOLOGY — 1968

● At the NHRA's Winternationals, Ford unleashes ten R-code 428 Cobra Jet powered Mustang fastbacks, from a total of 50 produced, and bombs Super Stock Eliminator. The SS/FA entry of Al "Batman" Joniac takes home the proverbial marbles. Only the best from the Ford Drag Team pilot these cars, including the likes of Gas Ronda, Hubert Platt, Jerry Harvey, "Dyno Don" Nicholson and Bill Lawton.

● On the big screen, Steve McQueen immortalizes the fictional detective

Frank Bullitt in the movie *Bullitt*. At the same time, he vaults a 390cu.in, four-speed equipped, Highland Green 1968 Mustang fastback to stardom in an unforgettable chase through San Francisco. And yes, McQueen does all his own stunt driving!

● The Mustang GT/CS, or California Special, as it is more commonly known, is released mid-year. It is an attempt to dress up a lowly Mustang coupe, using Shelby Mustang inspired fiberglass bolt-ons. And it works! Cal Specials are sold in record numbers

and duly become some of the most collectible of early Mustangs.

● Carroll Shelby opens a Ford dealership in Lake Tahoe, Nevada. He sells the "Shelby" trade name to Ford, but later is freed from this agreement.

● Also mid-year, the Cobra Jet Mustang GT is released, being a streetable version of the notorious 428 CJ drag car.

● About the same time, Shelby's GT-500KR (King of the Road) debuts.

Above left and left **In mid-1968, in an attempt to shore up sagging sales of entry-level cars, the Western Region Ford dealers took their cue from the Rocky Mountain Region HCS and, inspired by Carroll Shelby's Little Red and Green Hornet cars, created the Mustang GT/CS. These San Jose, California assembled coupes featured both Interior and Exterior Decor Trim Group options as standard, along with special bodywork, including the ever popular sequential taillights. They could also be ordered with almost any of the available engines, although the 302 was by far the most common. Today, these cars are very collectible, especially six-cylinder and big-block models.**

37

1969 Mustang SportsRoof 2+2. Ford's Going Thing Group says the new Mustang is the sportiest, go'ngest thing on wheels for '69.

The very first Mustang, most successful new car in history. For 4 years, nobody's been able to beat it.

1969 MUSTANG. All new. And like nothing in the neighborhood. ▪ For '69 it's longer, wider and heftier, too. Really hugs the road. Roomier than ever. It's a convertible. Or hardtop. Or SportsRoof. It's up to you, with 5 great models to choose from, including 2 you've never even heard of: the elegant Grandé and super-red-hot Mach I. ▪ There are 4 new V-8's, including the sizzling 428 Cobra Jet. That raises your number of Mustang engine choices to 8. And your spirits to a new high. ▪ Go hot. Or cool. Or luxurious. Or sporty. Mix them or match them. Whatever your thing, Mustang's ready with the model, the power, the options you need. At your kind of price. That's the kind of car Mustang is: very satisfying.

MUSTANG   *Ford*

FORD It's the going thing!

Somebody finally built a better Mustang.

CHAPTER 3

BEAUTY AND THE BEAST: 1969-70

In the fall of 1968, Ford Division effectively silenced the critics who claimed that the 1967-68 Mustangs were little more than facelifted renditions of America's first ponycar, by introducing a boldly styled, all-new 1969 Mustang. And what a Mustang it was!

If the aggressive front of the 1969 Mustang model provoked memories of the 1967 Shelby, it was by no means coincidental. Ever since the Shelby program's inception, Ford's Marketing Department, and Advanced Styling Studios had been using the limited-production model as a guinea pig, field testing a series of bold styling and engineering concepts. The response, or input, from these programs gave the manufacturer a valuable insight into the minds of the most discerning of ponycar enthusiasts.

The 1969 Mustang was so striking in appearance that no one seemed to mind the fact that it was by far the largest version to date, being a full 4in longer than its predecessor. Aside from its bold front end treatment, complete with optional scooped hood, the flanks of the new car featured a prominent pair of horizontal, parallel body lines, which ran from the top of the fender, adjacent to the headlight bucket, to the rear of the car. Here, they were reunited to form the flareline for the non-functional side scoops.

On both the coupe and SportsRoof (fastback) models, the new Mustang's roof line appeared racier than its forerunners, sporting a much swoopier profile. The tail was smoothed out, while the

Facing page and left
"Somebody finally built a better Mustang", and we couldn't agree more. The Mustang for 1969 was restyled from the ground up, again with three models to choose from. Its boldly accentuated grille cavity, swept fastback and clean side profile with integral spoiler made this car look like it was traveling at 200mph when it was standing still! With an assortment of configurations of the base car, and "5 great models to choose from", it was the Mustang that everyone had been waiting for.

SportsRoof boasted a kicked up, integral rear deck spoiler, which dared to be different. Its three-bar vertical taillights were in keeping with the overall design theme. On both the hardtop and convertible versions, a small, yet noticeable, accent line originated from the flared wheel lip opening and extended back to the foremost tip of the quarter panel, where it terminated just above the bumper recess.

Inside, Ford's new ponycar epitomized style and grace. An all-new, twin-pod crash pad featured a redesigned dual-quad instrument panel. This contained four gauges, which were recessed into the dash, a larger-diameter 120mph speedometer being located on the left of the steering column. On standard models, a combination fuel level/engine coolant gauge was located on the right, housed inside the larger-diameter gauge module. Last, but certainly not least, an oil pressure gauge could be found directly alongside it.

On Deluxe Interior Decor Group cars (SportsRoof or hardtop), an 8000rpm tachometer could be specified, while the instruments had gray faces with "idiot lights" to monitor vital engine functions. Furthermore, an electric clock was also available, although it was standard issue on upscale Mustangs, and was conveniently housed in the passenger-side gauge pod.

The 1969 Mustang featured a two-spoke steering wheel with a conventional half-moon horn ring as standard. However, a simulated-woodgrain, three-spoke Rim-Blow wheel was available as a deluxe option. Baseline cars had a fairly standard vinyl interior, sporting a pair of redesigned bucket seats. The previ-

Right **Southern Californian Tina New poses alongside a beautifully restored example of a 1969 Mach 1 Mustang.**

ously optional adjustable headrest was now listed as standard.

With a choice of Interior Decor Group and Deluxe Interior Decor Group options, the sky was the proverbial limit when it came to interior trim. The former provided comfortweave upholstery with knitted vinyl seat inserts. The latter included bucket seats with vinyl bolsters on each side.

High-back bucket seats were offered for the first time that year in both standard and deluxe configurations, being optional on all models except the Grande and Mach 1. Two styles of door panel were offered, the deluxe version sporting a woodgrain applique, moulded

armrest and running-horse motif. The Mustang for 1969 also featured a new full-length center console that incorporated an ash tray, a cigarette lighter and a combination padded armrest/map storage bin.

The list of powertrains began with a standard 200cu.in straight-six, backed by either a three-speed manual or C-4 automatic transmission, followed by a 250cu.in six. Cars equipped with these engines came with either a 3.00:1 (200cu.in) or 2.79:1 (250cu.in) rear end gear ratio, encased in an 8in live axle. Brakes were the four-wheel drum variety, with 14x5in, four-lug, safety-rim steel wheels. Suspension on the base-

line model was basically a carry-over from the previous year.

The Mustang's entry-level V-8 was a 210hp, 302cu.in 2-V package, available with the same transmissions, gear ratios and suspension package as the six-banger.

Next up was the all-new, canted-valve, four-bolt-mains, 290hp Boss 302, which could only be installed in the racy model bearing the same name. The Boss package featured a medium-riser aluminum intake manifold with a Holley 4-V carburetor, 6000rpm rev limiter, dual-point distributor, dual Thermactor exhaust, Top Loader four-speed transmission, 3.50:1-geared nodular 9in rear end, competition

Below **This gatefold advertisement, was published in** *Hot Rod* **magazine and not only featured high-performance versions of the Mustang (pictured is a Candy-apple red Mach 1), but also, on a second page, the mid-size Fairlane, Torino and Cobra models.**

Right **Ford was mighty proud of the fact that speed king Mickey Thompson had used Mustangs to break 295 speed and endurance records on Bonneville Salt Flats. As a result, the company ran this advertisement in the December 1968 issue of *Motor Trend*.**

suspension package incorporating staggered rear shocks, Magnum 500 wheels and, of course, a distinctive Boss 302 appearance group. The Boss 302 was certainly the true hot rod of the 1969 Mustang range.

Then, for the first time, came the 351 Windsor, a grown-up version of the 302 V-8, which was available in both 250hp, 2-V and 290hp, 4-V versions. The 351-W/2-V could be ordered across the board, but the 4-V model could only be specified in the Mustang GT and the newly introduced Mach 1. A choice of four-speed manual, or C-4 or C-6 automatics was offered. Rear end ratios ranged from 2.75:1 to 4.30:1, in either

Right **Shown at speed is another of Mickey Thompson's more successful endeavors: his famed Mach 1 AA/Funny Car.**

8 or 9in configurations, while competition suspension and power assisted front disc/rear drum brakes were standard.

The 320hp, 390cu.in FE was the next engine on the list, being offered in 4-V form only. It was available in all models except the Boss, and could be ordered with either a four-speed manual transmission or C-6 automatic. Cars sporting the 390 FE engine option also came with heavy-duty suspension and gear ratios from 2.75:1 to 4.30:1 inside their staggered-shocked, 9in rear axles.

The overwhelming response to the Cobra Jet factory race car project led to the introduction of a 335hp version of the 428, in either standard 4-V or Cobra Jet Ram Air configurations. The 428 package was also made available across the board, backed by either a Top Loader four-speed or beefed-up C-6. Rear end gears had ratios ranging from 3.25:1 to 4.30:1 and were contained in heavy-duty, 9in nodular-iron housings.

Last, but not least, was the limited-edition Boss 429. The 375hp, 735cfm Holley equipped, canted-valve, semi-hemi-head Boss 429, or Shotgun motor, as it was also known, was originally intended for NASCAR competition. However, for this beast to be homologated for super speedway competition, it had to be a production-line item. No problem! Ford and the Kar Kraft Corporation, of Brighton, Michigan, simply built 500 specially outfitted (read that, "hand assembled") Mustang SportsRoofs bearing the same name. Officially known as the NASCAR Mustang project or 429 HO project, the

Below **This ad proclaimed: "Nearest thing to a Trans-Am Mustang that you can bolt a license plate onto." With the Boss 302, that was actually the case.**

Boss 429 came with a heavy-duty Top Loader four-speed transmission equipped with a Hurst shifter. It had competition suspension, incorporating heavy-duty Gabriel shocks and a sturdy anti-sway bar, while the front brakes were power assisted 11in discs. Gearing in the 9in Traction Lok rear axle was 3.91:1.

Over in the Shelby camp, everything was brand new once more. The car's styling produced one of the most attractive of all the Shelbys, thanks to its wide mouth, NACA-ducted Ram Air fiberglass hood, side scoops and sequential taillight panel. A set of 15x7in Motor Wheel Corporation five-spoke wheels with Goodyear Polyglas GT F-60 rubber was also part of the package.

While suspension options were basically the same as the previous year, engine packages differed slightly. Gone was the 302 V-8, and in its place was a 290hp 4-V 351-W, complete with Paxton supercharger option on the GT-350. Exponents of the GT-500 could order the 335hp Ram Air 428 CJ package, sporting a 735cfm Holley 4-V carburetor, Shelby aluminum medium-rise intake, dual-point distributor, and finned aluminum Shelby valve covers. Both models could be ordered with either a Top Loader four-speed or C-6 transmission.

Mildly restyled for '70

Ford's 1970 Mustang line was basically a mildly restyled version of the previous year's range. Save for the deletion of the simulated side scoops, the relocation of the headlights to the inside of the grille cavity, the slight recessing of the taillights into the rear panel, and the addition of an extruded aluminum lower rocker panel on the Mach 1, it could have been the same car. But that wasn't necessarily a bad thing, for in terms of

Above **J.Walter Thompson was the best when it came to creating "image ads" such as this one. Despite the wording, the photograph clearly shows a supercharged 427 SOHC powered Top Fuel Dragster. No problem; it still worked.**

Right **The real thing: a perfect example of the rare Boss 429.**

MUSTANG CHRONOLOGY — 1969

● Ford introduces four new Mustang models: Mach 1, Grande, Boss 302 and Boss 429.

● After losing the 1968 SCCA Trans-Am championship to the factory sponsored Donahue/Penske/Sunoco Camaro team, Ford counters with two factory teams. The Shelby Racing Company fields two Kar Kraft prepared Boss 302 Mustangs, while NASCAR's Bud Moore Engineering runs two similarly prepared Boss 302s. In the end, Bud Moore drivers George Follmer and Parnelli Jones barely lose the championship to Penske/Donahue's Sunoco Camaro.

● Providence, Rhode Island Ford dealer Bob Tasca hits the drag strips with an 11-second, aluminum-block, 494cu.in Boss 429 Mustang, fittingly named "Super Boss". It's a beauty.

● Ford introduces an economy six-cylinder standard SportsRoof, named the Mustang E, but does little to promote it.

● Land speed record king Mickey Thompson fields a pair of tube-chassised, supercharged, nitromethane burning, 427 SOHC Mach 1 Funny Cars, and wins practically everything in sight. At Bonneville, Mickey sets a host of records with a trio of Mustangs: a Boss 302, a 427 SportsRoof and a 428 tunnel-port SportsRoof. Late in the season, he also debuts a Pro Stock Boss 429 driven by Butch Leal.

● Late in 1969, Ford and Kar Kraft build two Quarter Horse prototype Mustangs, one Candy-apple red and the other Grabber blue. These cars are used for feasibility studies and incorporate parts from the Boss and Shelby Mustangs, and the Mercury Cougar. The blue car features a Boss 429, while the red example has a 429 CJ engine. Both still exist and are in the hands of private collectors.

● Ford drops the Shelby and GT from production. The remaining Shelbys are redesignated 1970 models.

Above and above left
"Fire & Refinement" was the punchline of this advertisement touting Carroll Shelby's 1969 GT-350 and GT-500 Mustangs.

Above and above right
Two very different approaches were employed in these advertisements. The first, "Number One, there's Mustang", appears to be more fashion oriented. The second, "Mach 1—pronounced Mach Won!", trades on the car's obvious performance attributes.

Right **For 1970, the Mach 1 Mustang was given a distinctive aluminum lower rocker panel.**

46

sales, the 1969 Mustang had done quite well for itself.

Minor interior changes, such as to the instrumentation, were also made. A new feature for the 1970 models was a lockable steering column.

Upscale versions of the 1970 Mustang were offered in a series of eye popping "Grabber" colors (yellow, green, blue and orange), while a total of 11 power-trains was available. An addition to the engine list was the brand-new 351 Cleveland, which was a direct descendant of the Boss 302 family.

As already mentioned, 1970 would be the last year for the Shelbys. Poor sales figures were cited, as the cars were the most expensive Mustangs of all and faced stiff competition, not only from the "Brand-X" contingent, but also from other Mustangs, like the Mach 1, Boss 302 and Boss 429.

MUSTANG CHRONOLOGY — 1970

● Ford announces a drastic cutback in competition activities, terminating its racing contract with Shelby. The agreement with Bud Moore Engineering is renewed, however, and the team fields a pair of gold Boss 302 Trans-Am cars. The primary drivers are Follmer and Jones, who dominate the SCCA Trans-Am series.

● Detroit lawyer, and former Plymouth factory team driver, Al "The Lawman" Eckstrand creates the Lawman Performance Team, based on a highly modified Boss 429 Mustang, and tours US military bases in the Pacific and Europe. The project receives official blessing from Ford and Goodyear.

● American Raceways Incorporated, owners of Michigan International Speedway, Atlanta Motor Speedway, Texas International Raceway, Riverside International Raceway and

the yet-to-be-constructed Eastern International Raceway, contracts with Ford to use 20 Mustangs as official pace cars. Five are 428 Cobra Jet Mach 1s, another five special R-code 428 CJ convertibles, while the remainder are standard 302 SportsRoofs. Fortunately, a large number of these cars have been saved for posterity and are in the hands of collectors.

● Famed Michigan drag racer Connie Kalitta debuts a Boss 429 powered, nitromethane burning Mustang Funny Car and Top Fuel Dragster for quarter-mile competition.

● Ford launches the Mustang Grabber SportsRoof economy model.

● Boss 302 and Boss 429 models are phased out of production.

Survival of the fittest: Mustang is America's No.1 sporty car again.

MUSTANG *Ford*

Above With a reputation to be gained on the street, this ad plays on the age-old tag line, "Survival of the fittest". The sporty Mach 1 was a winner all the way.

'71 Mustang. New Style and Handling from the Trans-Am Winner.

Mustang has always meant outstanding roadability and nimble handling. Proof comes from three Trans-Am and two SCCA National Rally Championships.

And 1971 brings you even more Mustang. Wider tread. Lower stance. All-new body-chassis. Super slippery Sports-Roof. New optional 351 Boss HO and 429 CJ-R 4V V-8's with Dual Ram induction. And improved handling that *MOTOR TREND* describes as " . . . a definite tendency to hug the road much tighter in cornering."

Mach I has the pole position. Standard thin-wall 302 V-8, all-synch 3-speed floor shift, low restriction honeycomb grille, sport lamps, tuned competition suspension with high rate springs, shocks and stabilizer bars, E70-14 belted tires, color-keyed spoiler bumper, dual racing mirrors, High Back buckets, more. With options to match.

Go for the action. Test one of the six new Mustang models today at your Ford Dealer's. Find out which of these great road cars is for you.

MUSTANG MACH I

MUSTANG *Ford*

Right **This advertisement appeared in the December 1970 issue of** *Motor Trend* **and traded on the Mustang's 1970 SCCA Trans-Am championship victory, proclaiming: "New style and handling from the Trans-Am winner." It went on to list the available models, powertrains and options.**

48

CHAPTER 4

BIGGER IS BETTER?: 1971-73

By 1971, the Mustang again experienced growing pains, the wheelbase having been expanded to 109in. Apparently, the styling had been influenced by the cubist school, since this was the boxiest ponycar of all time. Federal regulations also led to the inclusion of 5mph safety bumpers and steelguard, safety-beam doors.

Gone were the Boss 302 and Boss 429, but in their place was the Boss 351, powered by the four-bolt-mains, 330hp, Ram Air 351 SCJ Cleveland motor. This package offered a choice of four-speed manual transmission or C-6 automatic. The Boss 351 also came with blackout Ram Air hood, upscale interior, reflective side stripes, rear deck spoiler, competition suspension and Magnum 500 styled steel wheels.

While the Boss 351 Cleveland unit was new, Ford pared down the engine option list from the previous year's 11 powerplants to eight. The 145hp, 250cu.in straight-six was made standard on the 1971 base model. Next came the 210hp, 2-V 302 V-8, followed by three non-Boss 351-C engine packages producing 240-285hp, all available in the baseline cars, Mach 1 and Grande. Big-block enthusiasts could opt for either the non-Ram Air, 370hp 4-V or 375hp, 4-V Ram Air set-up available in the Mach 1.

As before, transmission choices comprised the baseline three-speed, Top Loader four-speed, C-4 and C-6. Both 8 and 9in rear axles were available, the latter being standard in the performance models. Final gear ratios varied from 2.79:1 to 4.11:1.

1972: The end in sight
Whether Mustang enthusiasts realized it or not, by 1972, the proverbial writing was on the wall. The contemporary Mustang's days were numbered, and rumors abounded of a new, and decidely different, type of Mustang that was waiting in the wings. No longer available were the Boss 351 and 429 SCJ Mach 1 models. Rising insurance premiums for so called musclecars, nationwide safety regulations, and competition from the "Brand-X" contingent had left the Mustang's ranks decimated.

Still, a small ray of hope remained: it

Left **A 285hp, 4-V 351 Cleveland powered, Candy-apple red Mach 1 from 1971.**

was called the Mach 1. For 1972, the Mach 1 Mustang featured a 275hp, low-compression, unleaded-fuel, Autolite 4-V 351 High Output engine package. This was available with either a Top Loader four-speed or a C-6 automatic. The car also featured heavy-duty, staggered-shock suspension, power assisted front disc brakes, a 3.91:1 Traction Lok rear end and Magnum 500 wheels. Of course, the distinctive Appearance Group was standard, which was a saving grace, since it distinguished the car from the rest of that year's unexciting ponycar line.

The Grande was offered once again to the low-performance Mustang buyer, and appeared to be even plusher than before. Ford also introduced yet another springtime special, named the Sprint Decor Option. In fact, this Mustang was one of a highly publicized trio of Fords, the others being a Maverick and a Pinto. These thinly disguised baseline models were patriotically decked out in red, white and blue, with blue cloth and white vinyl interiors.

Unlike previous springtime editions, however, the new Mustang was offered with any available engine, although most examples featured the 136hp, 2-V 302 V-8. Furthermore, the Sprint Decor Option Mustang could be ordered with 15in Magnum 500 wheels, F60x15in Goodyear Polyglas rubber and competition suspension. Initial sales were not

Above **This rare magazine advertisement touts the 1971 limited-edition Mustang coupe: "For Spring Only. A Mustang of a New Stripe." This model featured a hood with NACA-style ducted scoops, Boss side graphics, blackout side paint treatment, and color keyed urethane spoiler.**

Right **The one-year-only 1971 Boss 351 Mustang.**

MUSTANG CHRONOLOGY — 1971

● Ford debuts the canted-valve 351 Cleveland engine, so named because of its origins in the Cleveland engine plant. The 351-C is offered in several configurations: 240hp, 2-V; 285hp, 4-V; 280hp, 4-V non-Ram Air; and a 330hp, 4-V Ram Air SCJ package.

● Sean Connery, playing special agent James Bond in the movie *Diamonds Are Forever*, outruns the bad guys in a red 1971 Mach 1

Mustang, in a chase scene through Las Vegas, Nevada. In reality, members of the Joie Chitwood Thrill Show do all the driving, including their famous two-wheel tilt stunt.

● Ford introduces the economy Sports Hardtop coupe. With Mach 1 grille, color keyed front bumper, NACA-ducted hood, Boss 351 side stripes and semi-gloss black rocker panels, it draws buyers aplenty.

Above **This ad simply stated: "Mustang, it's a personal thing." That it certainly was. The pewter-colored SportsRoof is of particular interest, as this hue was offered for the first time in the 1971 model.**

Left **A fine example of the 1971 SCJ Mach 1.**

Below and right **These advertisements encourage potential new car purchasers to "put a little Sprint" in their lives by purchasing a Mustang, Pinto or Maverick Sprint Special Edition. One also promotes the sense of control, balance and style that comes with owning a Mustang Sprint.**

Far right **This ad also stresses control and balance, comparing driving a Mustang to sailing. The analogy may be a bit far fetched, but nonetheless it's a classy looking production.**

encouraging, which is not surprising in view of the fact that the model was little more than a marketing upgrade.

Getting ready for a change

That familiar line, "the party's over", best summed up the Mustang for 1973. Ford had already announced that a new car, the Mustang II, was waiting in the wings to take over.

Although the models (except the Sprint Decor Option) and powertrains remained virtually the same, Ford did have the decency to freshen these cars cosmetically. They received a re-designed grille and taillight panel, a new upscale wheel package and federally-mandated, 5mph front safety bumper.

Options ranged from an Exterior Decor Group to special Metallic Glow paint. It was all too apparent, however, that Ford was using up its remaining inventory of parts in readiness for the impending changeover to the new model.

MUSTANG CHRONOLOGY — 1972-73

● During 1972, rumors abound concerning the Mustang's imminent replacement, said to be anything from a Torino-sized intermediate to a subcompact based on the Pinto.

● For 1973, apart from minor cosmetic changes, little is done to upgrade the Mustang; Ford is concentrating on the Mustang II.

This page Once more, promotional models played an important role in the Mustang's history. A 1/25-scale, Yellow Gold, AMT manufactured Mach 1 dealer promotional model is shown alongside a similarly-hued, 1/64-scale Corgi Toys Mach 1 from the same era (*top*). Youngsters could also purchase this Rusher Mach 1 tin toy for a couple of dollars at the local store (*left*).

CHAPTER 5

A DIFFERENT KIND OF MUSTANG: 1974-78

If Ford ever believed in shock tactics, the company certainly used them to the full in the fall of 1973, with the introduction of the down-sized Mustang II. Resulting from pressure by both state and federal governments, and the insurance industry, the Mustang II was not a traditional ponycar in performance terms, but it was "politically correct" for the times. However, in the eyes of Mustang traditionalists, the car was nothing more than a glamorized version of the subcompact Pinto, on which it was based. Not surprisingly, they were far from amused.

The basis for the new Mustang was the Pinto's 94.2in-wheelbase platform, which featured rack-and-pinion steering, unequal-length upper and lower control arms, coil-spring front suspension, and parallel-leaf-spring rear suspension supporting a normal live axle. The styling was to be reminiscent of earlier Mustangs, yet contemporary enough to sell in large volume.

The "dwarf Mustang", as it was quickly labeled, featured all the traditional styling cues of its predecessors: open-mouth grille, simulated side scoops and fastback styling. However, they were integrated into a compact, fuel-efficient and insurable package. The initial impression often given by the car was:

"Gee, when I grow up, I want to be a REAL Mustang!"

Perhaps the greatest shock to Mustang aficionados was the fact that the 1974 Mustang II was launched without a single V-8 engine option for either the coupe or fastback models. In fact, only two engine packages were available. Powering the entry-level "Pinto-Stang" was an 87hp, 2.3-liter, OHC, four-cylinder engine, with a choice of four-speed manual or three-speed

Cruise-O-Matic transmissions. This was followed by a 97hp, 2.8-liter V-6 with the same transmission options. Talk about culture shock.

Mustang II models came in standard, Ghia and luxury Silver Ghia (sort of a down-sized Grande) versions. Later an MPG package was introduced and, believe it or not, there was also a V-6 Mach 1. Despite the disappointment in the Mustang II, it was still a pretty good car, or at least it was representative of its

Left **An AMT 1/25-scale, plastic dealer promo model of the 1974 Mustang II, its underside boasting all the appropriate engineering features of the new car.**

Right **This commemorative copper coin was given away by Ford dealers. On one side, it shows a 1965 Mustang coupe with a pony in the background, and bears the legend: "The right car at the right time." On the other side is a prancing pony and a 1974 Mustang II. What a collectible this is!**

Right **In this 1975 advertisement for the Mach 1 and Ghia models, virtually all the dealer options are listed. High priority is given to the new 133hp 302 V-8.**

time. In fact, *Motor Trend* named the introductory model Car of the Year.

V-8 again

In 1975, Ford responded to the pleas of shocked Mustang traditionalists by putting a 302 V-8 back into its ponycar product line. This engine was offered in both 129 and 133hp, 2-V versions, the latter being employed in the Mach 1 in place of the V-6. That powerplant remained available, however, as did the entry-level 2.3 OHC four-banger. They were equipped with the same transmission options.

The best on offer

While Ford missed the proverbial boat in 1976, by not offering a bicentennial Mustang II package to commemorate the 200th anniversary of the United States of America, at least the company did hit the mark — unless you look at it from the Shelby Cobra enthusiast's viewpoint — with the release of the

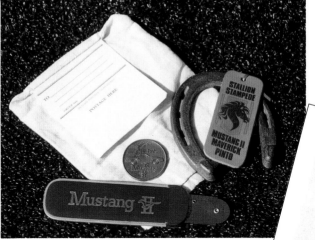

This page **The Stallion Stampede advertising campaign, of 1976, was based on Ford's successful formula of promoting cosmetically packaged entry-level models. As can be seen, many promotional items, including this dealer's survey horseshoe, were given away.**

sporty Cobra II. However, while this model did boast a 134hp 302 V-8, together with a four-speed manual transmission and a special wheel/tire/suspension package, it was also endowed with some of the most garish tape graphics ever conceived by man. Nonetheless, it was still the best that Ford had to offer ponycar fans.

The powerplant range that year comprised the 92hp, 2.3-liter four, the 100hp, 2.8-liter V-6 and the aforementioned V-8. Also offered was the unheralded Mustang II Stallion trim package, which included black and silver paint, aluminum wheels and special horse-head decals.

T-tops and sunroofs

Back again for 1977 were both the Mach 1 and Cobra II, offered this time with the popular T-Top option. A coupe with a sunroof was also available, along with a special Sports Appearance Group option for the Ghia. This consisted of a

57

This page **These ads traded heavily on the Shelby image, the 1976 Cobra II package being likened to the original Shelby GT-350 Mustang** (*below*)**. Shelby aficionados were not the least bit impressed. The "Mustang II. Bordom Zero" advertisement** (*right*) **brought to mind the 1966 Hertz GT-350H.**

wheel/tire package, and a whole host of color keyed components and stick-ons.

1978: Last of the Mustang IIs

Once you got past the tape graphics of the Cobra II, it was a pretty good car. The same could also be said of the Mach 1. And if that wasn't enough, the last of the Mustang IIs witnessed the introduction of the King Cobra package, complete with 302 V-8, four-speed, cast-aluminum wheels, power assisted steering and special interior.

As sport compacts go, the Mustang II was excellent, but it was unleashed on an unsuspecting high-performance car market at the worst possible moment.

MUSTANG II CHRONOLOGY – 1974-78

● On its introduction, the Mustang II leaves ponycar traditionalists shell shocked through the lack of a V-8 engine option. Even so, *Motor Trend* magazine votes it Car of the Year.

● IMSA racer Charlie Kemp builds a one-off Trans-Am Mustang II. NHRA Pro Stock competitors "Dyno Don" Nicholson, Gapp & Roush and Bob Glidden field big-engine Mustang IIs. NHRA's Funny Car classes all but adopt the Mustang II as the official

body style of the nitro burning category in quarter-mile competition.

● In keeping with the budget-package Mustang tradition, Ford introduces an MPG model by the end of 1974.

● Actress Farrah Fawcett, as Sabrina in the hit TV show *Charlie's Angels*, routinely chases the bad guys in a blue-striped, white Mustang Cobra II.

● Ford introduces the Stallion

Stampede package in conjunction with the Pinto and Maverick. These are economy offerings brightened up with special graphics.

● *Hot Rod* magazine and Monroe Shock Absorber Corporation create the Monroe Handler Mustang II, complete with Trans-Am body kit, engine mods, and fat wheels and tires.

● JWT devises a "Mustang II, Boredom Zero" ad campaign in 1977.

Right **This advertisement proudly proclaimed: "Introducing The New Breed. Ford Mustang '79". It was unusual in that it was strictly a visual presentation, allowing the product to speak for itself.**

60

CHAPTER 6

THE FOX AND THE HOUNDS: 1979-93

After what seemed an eternity of ponycar mediocrity, the Mustang II era officially came to a screeching halt in early October 1978, with the introduction of the completely new Fox Mustang. Ford Division's third-generation ponycar would launch an exciting new era of domestically produced, "consumer-friendly" cars based on the popular "World Class" building concept. Starting with the 1979 Mustang, each new Ford model would firmly embrace the aesthetically-pleasing "Euro look", which was becoming established around the world.

In the main, the credit for styling Ford's first aerodynamic ponycar belongs to the company's chief stylist John J. "Jack" Telnack, along with Fritz Mayhew (creator of the original Mustang's red, white and blue, three-bar, running-horse emblem), Bob Zokas and Tosho Saito.

The Mustang for 1979 featured a bold, wind cheating, wrap-around sloping front panel, manufactured from pliable polyurethane plastic and concealing a 5mph safety bumper. Its egg-crate grille was flanked by two pairs of square, sealed-beam headlights, along with a pair of amber turn-signal/driving lights located directly below. In addition, there was a vertical amber parking light at each side.

Each flank featured a trio of horizontal body accent lines, which ran from headlight to taillight, along with flush mounted door handles and a 2in, dent-resistant, polyurethane body band, or safety door guard. In keeping with the advanced aerodynamic principles currently in

Left **The third generation of Mustang brought a completely new "European" look to ponycar styling.**

vogue, the new Mustang featured a raked windshield, while expansive side glass offered maximum visibility. On three-door fastback models, the rear body pillars flowed into either a hatchback or trunk design. Out back, there were three-bar vertical taillights and a clear plastic back-up light panel, which concealed the 5mph safety bumper.

Based on a 100.5in-wheelbase, multi-layered-sheetmetal platform, the exciting new ponycar (with the project code name "Fox") boasted technologically advanced MacPherson strut-type front suspension, in which each front shock absorber and spindle assembly were combined to form a single component.

The upper suspension pickup points were located at the very top of what had been known as the shock towers in the Mustang II, while the bottom of each MacPherson strut was attached to a lower control arm. When combined with a pair of specific-rate coil springs and a 12mm anti-sway bar, this front suspension arrangement helped provide the Mustang with handling that could be considered truly world class.

The rear suspension comprised a set of horizontally-opposed, torque-box-mounted, unequal-length, upper and lower trailing arms; two constant-rate coil springs; a pair of mono-tube hydraulic shock absorbers; and a 1.06in-

diameter anti-sway bar. These worked in unison to effectively plant the Mustang's 7.5in live rear axle (with ratios spanning 3.08:1 to 2.47:1) firmly on the tarmac in myriad driving conditions.

Rolling stock on the third-generation Mustang consisted of 13x5.5in or 14x5.5in, four-lug, stamped steel safety rims with a choice of standard or deluxe wire-type hubcaps. Upscale models (Cobra, Pace Car, etc) came with a special Michelin metric wheel and tire package, comprising 15.35x5.9in aluminum wheels shod with 190/65R390 TRX Kevlar/steel-belted radial tires. Stopping was accomplished by a pair of 10in, four-lug, dual-piston, vented front disc brakes and a pair of 9in, four-lug rear drum brakes.

The new Mustang debuted with a baseline 2.3-liter, OHC four-banger powerplant. Next was a 250cu.in six, as well as the more popular 2.8-liter Cologne 90-degree V-6. After that came two versions of the trusty 5.0-liter (302) V-8, both in 2-V configuration. Transmission choices for 1979 comprised three- and four-speed SROD stick-shifts, and the ever popular C-4 automatic.

Creature comforts inside included a recessed instrument cluster, housed in a sculpted foam crash pad and featuring an 80mph speedometer, 6000rpm tachometer and fuel, amps, water temperature and oil pressure gauges. One of the more interesting accoutrements was the sensory map warning light feature, located on the console, directly below the push-button AM/FM radio-cassette. This novelty consisted of an overhead schematic of the car with red and green warning lights at strategic locations. These would illuminate when

Right **A unique silk-screened metal serving tray that utilizes the same image as the ad on page 60. It has the Mustang history on the reverse.**

ems were detected, warning the
r of any systems malfunction.

the front, there was a pair of manu-
adjusted, semi-reclining bucket
s, Recaros being standard equip-
in Indy Pace Car, Cobra and Turbo
a models. Behind these, all models
a bench seat, which could be folded
ı on three-door versions.

1979, the Mustang was available
ther a notchback coupe or a three-
hatchback, leaving convertible fans
bit of a loss. As far as specific mod-
were concerned, there was the
ang L, LX, Ghia, Cobra, Turbo
a and Indianapolis 500 Pace Car.

e Indy 500 Pace Car package was
popular, thanks to its distinctive
er, black and orange graphics,
elin TRX handling package, hounds-
-patterned Recaro seats, machine
d aluminum dash, and choice of
r a Garrett AiResearch turbo-
ged, 2.3-liter OHC four or a 5.0-liter
Approximately 11,000 of these spe-
models were produced, a total of 78
Cars being used for the actual run-
of the 63rd annual event. Without
tion, the Indianapolis 500 Mustang
Car of 1979 became the very first
ctible late-model Mustang.

wever, the Mustang Cobra and
ang Turbo Cobra could not claim
same distinction. In essence, both
were quite similar to the Indy 500
el, having their own graphic pack-
. The same powertrain options were
able, yet for some reason, they
d to stimulate the interest of the
tang loyalist like the Pace Car.
y, pristine examples of either car
nand respectable prices.

this point, it should be noted that

Left **Radio Shack's radio controlled replica of a 1979 Mustang Cobra, produced that same year.**

Below **Technical freaks probably appreciated this** *Motor Trend* **advertisement, entitled "Sound The Charge", which addressed many of the Fox Mustang's engineering high points.**

Right **The high point of 1979 was Ford's participation in the 63rd running of the famed Indianapolis 500. Ford blanketed the country with myriad promotional items. Shown here are pristine examples of an Indy 500 Pace Car product information booklet, a Pace Car jacket, Indy 500 Pace Car metal serving tray, Monogram 1/25-scale Indy 500 Pace Car model, and Ezra Brooks Indy 500 Pace Car ceramic bourbon bottle.**

Below **The 1979 Pace Car replica is extremely collectible today.**

Ford Division generated more promotional material that year than ever before. Over 300 promotional items (jackets, hats, patches, T-shirts, pins, models, go-karts, postcards, decals, etc) were produced to help launch the new model. After four years of the Mustang II, some may have assumed that Ford was attempting to compensate the Mustang aficionado. But on a more realistic note, it was probably because the company was proud of the all-new ponycar.

Maintaining the status quo

The Mustang saw few changes for 1980. For some reason, Ford elected to introduce a 115hp 4.2-liter (255cu.in) V-8 into the line as a "50-state" emissions-lega engine. To bolster the Cobra's saggin sales, various Indy Pace Car suspensio and body trim pieces were incorporated That year, a coupe with a simulated con vertible top, known as the Sport Top also appeared.

Top Cobra

In 1981, Ford (finally) incorporated th C&C designed Indy Pace Car T-to option into the Mustang product line The Cobra package would be the top-o the-range model.

The GT returns

The big news for 1982 was the re introduction of the Mustang GT with it HO 2-V small-block V-8 option, sportin 8.3:1-compression-ratio pistons and sin gle exhaust. This was advertised a developing 157hp. The package wa backed by an SROD four-speed manua transmission, while there was a wid choice of gear ratios for the 7.5in rea end, ranging from 2.73:1 to 3.08:1 i limited-slip and Traction-Lok configura tions. The GT also came with 10.06i power assisted front disc brakes and th Pace Car's TRX wheel and tire packag

Appearing for the last time would b the lackluster 4.2-liter V-8, and no on seemed to complain. The turbocharge 2.3-liter four was also dropped.

A ragtop again

Fresh-air freaks could rejoice at the re introduction of a Mustang convertible i 1983 (manufactured on a Cars Concepts sub-assembly line). This wa

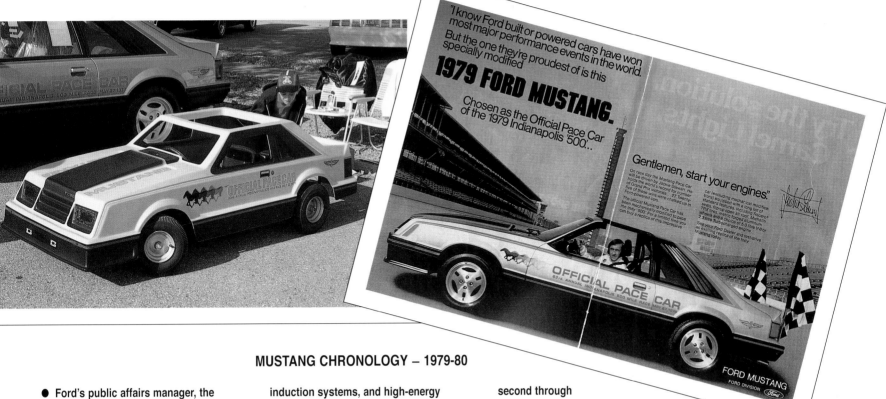

MUSTANG CHRONOLOGY – 1979-80

● Ford's public affairs manager, the late Paul Preuss, and new car product launch manager Chuck Gumushian, stage a mid-July sneak preview for select members of the automotive press at the Beverly Hills Hotel. While no car is present, editors are treated to an impressive slide show.

● Jack Roush Performance Engineering and Cars & Concepts win the contract to develop the Indianapolis 500 Pace Car prototypes. Roush prepares the suspension and powertrains, using fully blueprinted, 5.0-liter HO engines with Boss 302 crankshafts, special camshafts, reworked cylinder heads and

induction systems, and high-energy ignition systems. C&C produces the first T-top application, working closely with Ford's glass plant, and builds two Confirmed Prototype (CP) packages.

● Ford spokesman, and Indy 500 Grand Marshall, Jackie Stewart appears with the new Pace Car Mustang in a national advertising campaign touting the new model.

● Ford Division launches a Winner's Choice Sweepstakes contest through the automotive magazines, offering a Mustang Pace Car as one of the grand prizes, with an F-150 pickup, Fairmont Futura and Pinto Cruising Wagon as

second through fourth prizes.

● Rick Mears wins the Indy 500 for Penske. A Mustang Pace Car (which Mears still owns) is part of his prize.

● NHRA and IHRA Pro Stock drag racers "Dyno Don" Nicholson and Rickie Smith prepare Fox Mustang Pro Stockers for the 1979 campaign.

● In 1980, a limited-edition Firestone/McLaren HPR Mustang is introduced, sporting IMSA Trans-Am body panels and a turbocharged, OHC four-cylinder powerplant prepared by McLaren. Only 250 are produced.

Above **Official Indy 500 Grand Marshall Jackie Stewart kicked off the Pace Car project by posing for this gatefold advertisement.**

Above left **A flawless example of a Motor Sports Promotions, gasoline powered, Indy 500 Pace Car kart would command a lofty price in today's Pace Car collector market.**

offered with anything from a 2.3-liter four, through 2.6-liter V-6, to a Holley 4-V, 175hp, 5.0-liter powerplant. Initially, both three-speed, and SROD four-speed manual transmissions, plus the C-4 automatic, were available. By mid-year, however, the big news was the arrival of the Borg-Warner T-5 five-speed stick.

Still on board were the same TRX wheel/tire and suspension package options, which were standard on the GT.

Accent on high performance

The year 1984 is best remembered by Mustang enthusiasts world-wide as being a milestone of sorts, because Ford really focused on high performance, but with a considerably more sophisticated and technical approach than in previous years. The company's Special Vehicle Operations department (SVO), led by former Ford of Europe racing director Michael Kranefuss, jumped back into organized motorsports on a multitude of levels, ranging from NASCAR to NHRA, and IMSA to SCORE off-road racing.

On the new-car front, Ford unleashed its ultimate weapon, or "BMW killer", as it was often touted: the 1984½ Mustang SVO. This was the brainchild of Kranefuss and was developed by SVO chief engineer Glen S. Lyall. The Mustang SVO displayed strong European influences, but it was a Mustang nonetheless, albeit a cut above the ordinary ponycar.

With the exception of the basic unibody platform, the SVO shared little with its ponycar brethren. Beneath its offset-scooped hood lay the first electronically managed, multi-port fuel injected powerplant ever fitted to a Ford production vehicle. Featuring an 8.3:1 compression ratio, the 2.3-liter OHC four was equipped with a Garrett AiResearch turbocharger and intercooler (employing an integral wastegate) operating at a boost pressure of 14lb/sq.in. It pumped out 175hp and 210lb/ft torque. A handy, on-the-fly, driver-actuated fuel calibration switch could be used to wean the engine from a diet of premium fuel to lower-octane regular gas whenever the former could not be obtained.

Backing up this potent combination was the newly introduced Borg-Warner five-speed gearbox, replete with Hurst adjustable-stop, short-throw shifter. To

further the claim that the Mustang SVO was truly a driver's car, automatic transmission was not even considered when the specification was drawn up. And there were no apologies about that.

The SVO featured a quick-ratio, 20:1 (2.5 turns lock-to-lock), power assisted rack-and-pinion steering setup. Its MacPherson strut front suspension featured specially-designed gas-charged Koni shocks, a 1.12in-diameter anti-sway bar and forged-steel lower trailing arms. The rear suspension utilized a Koni Quadra-Shock setup to enhance cornering and reduce axle hop under hard acceleration. A much larger 0.67in

Left **This 1983 gatefold advertisement proclaimed: "The Boss: One Hot Piece of American Steel." That it certainly was! At this point, Ford was clearly in control of its high-performance destiny.**

Facing page, top **Ford Division went to great lengths to promote their exciting new car. Shown are two examples of 1979 Mustang coloring books, which posed the question to a future generation of Mustang buyers: "Have You Colored A Ford...Lately?"**

Facing page, bottom **In 1982, Ford and JWT heralded the re-release of the popular Mustang GT with its 2-V, 175hp 5.0-liter powerplant. It was really big news and warranted gatefold ads like this. Obviously, the excitement was back!**

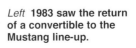

Left **1983 saw the return of a convertible to the Mustang line-up.**

This page **Hot news for 1984 was the Mustang SVO. With 2.3-liter, turbocharged, OHC four-banger, the SVO pumped out an honest 175hp at 5000rpm. Special Vehicle Operations engineers were rightfully proud of this accomplishment and posed for an ad entitled, "These are the men. This is the machine." Also shown is a Mustang SVO advertisement that appealed to the competitive spirit locked deep inside most American high-performance car enthusiasts.**

rear anti-sway bar was also standard SVO fare.

The braking system was a cut above the normal Mustang's, too, being upgraded to 11.08in-diameter, 1in-thick, five-lug, ventilated, dual-piston front disc brakes, with 11.6in-diameter discs bringing up the rear. A set of 16x7in aluma-cast, vented disc wheels were shod with low-profile P225/50VR Goodyear Gatorback rubber.

The SVO's interior was equally purposeful. It contained fully adjustable, lumbar-support Recaro bucket seats, normally trimmed in charcoal gray leather. The machine turned dash featured a 140mph analogue speedometer, an 8000rpm tachometer, a turbo boost gauge, an ammeter, and water temperature and oil pressure gauges. The steering wheel and shift knob were wrapped in leather, while there was a "dead pedal" footrest to the left of the floor.

Even the SVO's exterior differed from its siblings. The front panel contained larger sealed-beam halogen headlights, and nowhere to be seen was the familiar egg-crate grille. Everything had been smoothed out. The taillights also differed slightly from the other ponycars. Oh, and by the way, a Mustang SVO could cover the quarter mile in 15.5 seconds, producing a terminal speed of 137mph!

Another new arrival that year (although considerably less awe inspiring) was Ford's 20th-anniversary commemorative GT-350 Mustang. Actually, it could be said that whatever the SVO was, the GT-350 Mustang was not. Basically, it was a 205hp, carbureted 5.0-liter Mustang GT, featuring a specia

"20th Anniversary" shift knob and dash plaque, together with a set of red GT-350 side stripes, which were identical to those used on the 1966 Mustang GT. Both three-door and soft-top versions were offered, but they were only available in white.

Much to the chagrin of those who violated the nationally posted 55mph speed limit, they now had one more thing to worry about, besides astronomical insurance rates: Ford's Special Service Package, or Police Pursuit 5.0-liter Mustang notchback. These "Porsche chasers" could top 146mph and run for hours on end. They had uprated suspensions, Z-rated Goodyear Eagle uni-directional radial tires, and heavy-duty radiators, transmissions and oil coolers. First to employ them was the California Highway Patrol, who helped coin the somewhat humorous phrase: "Have you been chased by a Ford lately?"

The Mustang was also finding ready acceptance among special car builders. Leading the charge was road racer Steve Saleen. His first Mustangs were equipped with functional ground-effects panels, swoopy rear deck spoilers, trick graphics, and wheel, tire and brake upgrades. Their massaged carbureted 5.0-liter engines were capable of hurtling these "GT-350s for the nineties" to speeds in excess of 170mph.

Steady improvement

How do you top an act like 1984? Tough question! Rather than attempting to "fix what ain't broke", for 1985 Ford improved from within. For openers, the output of the HO 5.0-liter small-block V-8,

Left **With its aggressive front-end styling, the Mustang SVO looked every inch the "BMW killer" it was said to be.**

Above **The introduction of the Saleen Mustang, in 1984, echoed the Shelby's glory days, although the car was much more sophisticated. Saleen's early advertising urged buyers to "Experience the Adventure!"**

Right **Ford observed the Mustang's 20th anniversary by releasing the white-only, 20th-Anniversary GT-350, which was a thinly disguised Mustang GT. It was available in either three-door or convertible models. Shown is an example of the sales tag used to promote the car.**

MUSTANG CHRONOLOGY – 1984

● Fully electronic fuel injection (EFI) debuts on both 3.8-liter V-6 and 5.0-liter V-8 engine packages: a big step for Ford, and a first in the industry. The 5.0-liter High Output V-8 is also upgraded to 205hp.

● Ford's vice president of public affairs, Walter Hayes, convinces Henry Ford II that high performance sells cars in the eighties, and Ford's participation is essential. As a result, a Special Vehicle Operations (SVO) department is created.

● SVO and European speed merchant Zakspeed field an IMSA GTK Mustang Turbo, sponsored by Miller Beer and Ford Motorsport. Klaus Ludwig is the driver.

● In the middle of the year, the Mustang SVO debuts to rave reviews, being hailed as a "BMW killer". Ford ads proclaim: "Straight from the showroom, it's far from stock!"

● A racing version of the Mustang SVO is prepared by Bob Fehan. Sponsored by MAC Tools, it becomes a force to be reckoned with in IMSA's Camel GT class.

● The high-tech Mustang GTP IMSA race car is conceived, functioning not only as a racer, but also as a test bed for SVO, Ford Electronics and Ford Aerospace. Once again, Klaus Ludvig is one of the drivers. To everyone's delight, the GTPs place first and second on their first outing.

● Ford unveils the 20th-Anniversary GT-350 Mustang, but does little to promote it. Shelby loyalists are not even remotely amused.

● Even less popular is the Special Service Package police pursuit Mustang notchback. With long-range cruising capabilities and a top speed of 146mph, it generates an advertisement proclaiming: "This Ford chases Porsches for a living".

● Toward the end of the year, Ford and JWT produce an ad with the line: "Ford's Motorsports Strategy: Prove it here. Use it here." The advert features the notorious Mustang GTP, together with examples of the 1984 Thunderbird Turbo Coupe, Mustang SVO and EXP Turbo production cars.

● Formula Atlantic racer Steve Saleen borrows a page from Shelby American history by converting a mild-mannered Mustang GT into the first Saleen Mustang. With attractive ground effects, fine tuned suspension, trick wheels and tires, plus a "breathed on" 5.0-liter V-8, the Saleen Mustang is capable of 170mph and sells like hot cakes.

used in the Mustang GT, was upped by 5hp through the incorporation of a roller-cam valvetrain and two-speed accessory belt drive. That year, the upscale GT model also received variable-rate springs front and rear, along with a heavier anti-sway bar. Gone were those expensive-to-replace Michelin TRX wheels and tires; in their place, Ford substituted 15x7in Polycast finned-aluminum wheels, sporting Goodyear P225/60VR radials.

Also new was a welcome restyle of the nosecap. The 1985 car featured a more aerodynamic look, its slotted air intake opening being flanked by deeply recessed quad headlights, while a blue oval Ford badge was fitted above.

Even bigger news was the mid-year release of the 49-state-legal (sorry, California!) central fuel injection (CFI) 5.0-liter HO engine. This employed an electronically assisted throttle body instead of a carburetor.

The power rating of the SVO would also be increased from 175 to 205hp, achieved through cylinder head and camshaft revisions, a fuel injector upgrade and the use of dual exhausts. In addition, this model benefited from revised suspension and enhanced steering geometry, which improved handling. On the outside, the 1985 SVO also received flush mounted headlights.

Steve Saleen and his Saleen Mustangs were rapidly becoming hot

Left and above **Probably the best image builder for Ford's Special Vehicle Operations department was its two-year Mustang GTP IMSA race program. The Mustang GTP was a joint venture between SVO, Ford Aerospace and Ford Electronics. It appeared in a late-1984 advertisement that proclaimed: "Ford's Motorsports Strategy". This alluded to the link between the racer and Ford's "enthusiast" cars: the Thunderbird Turbo Coupe, the Mustang SVO and EXP Turbo.**

Right **This gatefold advertisement, looking down on a white 1985 Mustang convertible with a woman and swimming pool superimposed clearly borders on the sensual. But isn't that what high-performance road cars like the Ford Mustang are all about?**

topics. That year, he would offer a Paxton supercharger option, as well as a G-load brace for installing between the car's strut towers to help eliminate torsional body shift during hard cornering.

More improvements

For 1986, the welcome news for ponycar enthusiasts was the implementation of sequential electronic fuel injection (SEFI) on the Mustang's roller-cam V-8 engine. This arrangement consisted of a two-piece upper and lower intake, the intake runner serving as the bottom half (with eight 19lb Bosch fuel injectors installed), and an upper air plenum, complete with 60mm side-draft throttle body and EGR plate. This installation was governed by Ford's highly successful EEC-IV engine management system, which operated in conjunction with a speed density air meter.

Also new that year was a somewhat

MUSTANG CHRONOLOGY – 1985-86

● For 1985, the 4-V, 5.0-liter HO V-8 in the GT is upgraded with a roller-cam valvetrain and two-speed accessory belt drive. The power rating of the SVO is increased from 175 to 205hp.

● In mid-1985, Ford introduces 49-state-legal central fuel injection (CFI) on the 5.0-liter HO V-8.

● The Saleen Mustang enters its second year of production in 1985.

● Rumors abound that the next generation of Mustang will feature front-wheel drive. Mustang fans are outraged and demonstrate their anger by mailing over 30,000 letters of protest to Ford, prompting the company to change its marketing strategy. The proposed FWD Mustang actually becomes the Ford Probe.

● For 1986, sequential electronic fuel injection (SEFI) is introduced on the

5.0-liter HO V-8. Nitrogen-gas struts and shocks, and a heavier-duty rear axle also debut on V-8 models of the Mustang LX and GT.

● Much to Ford's delight, Steve Saleen's General Tire sponsored, two-car SCCA Escort Endurance Series race team (with Saleen and drivers Rick Titus, Desiree Wilson and Lisa Caceras) brings home FoMoCo's first manufacturer's championship in 1986.

ronger 8.8in version of the original rear
xle, packing gear ratios between 2.73:1
nd 3.27:1. Nitrogen-charged shocks
nd struts replaced the previous
ydraulic units, and the GT's rack-and-
nion steering was quickened up to a
tio of 15.01:1.

Much to the disappointment of SVO
vers, the power rating of the 1986
odel was reduced by 5hp to make the
ar more driveable in locales where
igh-octane fuel was at a premium.
ther than that, it received only minor
ody changes, including the installation
f a federally mandated third brakelight
the rear spoiler and an upgrade in
SVO" fender badging from a decal to
hrome block letters.

In 1986, Steve Saleen and his rene-
ade Mustangs also continued to show
heir winning ways, both off track and on.
owever, that year's model remained
irtually unchanged.

lo more SVO

luch to the chagrin of SVO enthusiasts,
ord deleted the model from its 1987
roduct line. Poor sales and competition
om within, waged by the cheaper 5.0-
ter Mustang LX and GT models, were
he car's ultimate downfall. Apart from
hat, everything was good news. The
lustang's pliable front panel presented
old fresh styling, with a much smoother
ose and flush mounted halogen head-
ght/parking lamp assemblies replacing
he quad headlights used on the previ-
us model.

The power rating of the 5.0-liter engine
vas increased by a full 25hp (225hp)
hrough the use of a free flowing, stain-
ess-steel dual exhaust system. That

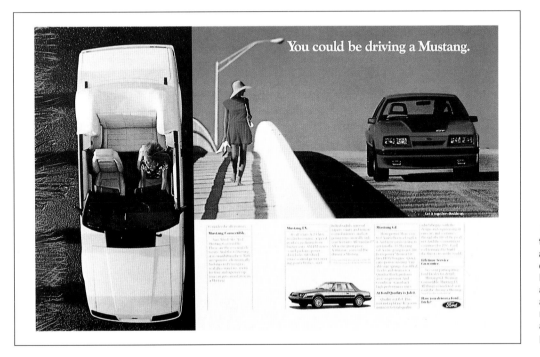

This page **Both of
these 1985 JWT
advertisements
clearly show the
Mustang's new
aerodynamic look
and extol the
respective models'
attributes in
precise terms.**

73

FORD MUSTANG Open Up and Say "Ahhh"

Above **This JWT advertisement touts the attributes of owning a 1988 Mustang convertible, which was available in either LX or GT trim. The simple tag line, "Open Up and Say 'Ahhh'", was effective.**

MUSTANG CHRONOLOGY – 1987-88

● The Mustang's "aero look" debuts with the 1987 product line, featuring a swoopy looking nose and a pair of flush mounted, single-unit halogen headlamps.

● The power rating of the 5.0-liter HO engine is increased from 200 to 225hp by fitting a revised exhaust system and tuning the engine management systems.

● Citing poor sales, Ford drops the Mustang SVO. The V-6 engine is also dropped from the Mustang line in '87.

● The ASC McLaren Mustang debuts, replacing the Fox-platform Mercury Capri previously used by the American Sunroof Company.

● The 2.3-liter OHC four is upgraded to electronic fuel injection, and is offered with the Borg-Warner T-5 manual transmission.

● The 1987 Saleen Mustang is tested in Lockheed Aircraft's wind tunnel during its initial design stages, producing an even swoopier model than before.

● Team Saleen maintains its grip on the SCCA Escort Endurance Series by annexing a second championship in 1987, followed by a third in 1988.

● Also that year, Roush Racing's IMSA GTO Mustangs achieve the team's first victory at the Daytona 24-hour endurance race.

year, the V-8 cars would also feature a 5lb spring increase in the front, along with an upgrade from the 10.06in vented front disc brake rotor to a slightly larger unit measuring 10.84in. Furthermore, Mustang LX models were updated with 14x7in, cast-aluminum slotted wheels, which would remain with that model until production ceased in 1993.

Also deleted from the production schedule was the 3.8-liter V-6 power-plant, while the baseline 2.3-liter OHC four-banger was converted to EFI. Moreover, for the first time, it was offered with the Borg-Warner five-speed manual transmission.

Little change

With all the changes to the previous year's model, it should come as no surprise that few alterations were made to the 1988 Mustang range. The only significant differences were the installation of a new 58-amp/hr heavy-duty battery, and a California-only mass airflow system (MAF).

Silver anniversary

With an apparent disregard for production milestones, Ford did little to celebrate the Mustang's 25th anniversary. However, all Mustangs manufactured between April 17, 1989 and April 17, 1990 had a small plastic, three-bar, running-horse emblem on the dash, which bore the legend: "25 years". When it came to options, power windows and door locks seemed to be the big news for 1989.

Fortunately for Saleen Mustang fans, Steve Saleen recognized an opportunity when it arose. His limited-edition, 25th-anniversary SSC was the silver-anniversary Mustang that Ford should have built. Sporting a federally certified 5.0-liter V-8 with ported and polished cylinder heads, 65mm throttle body, large-tube headers, and an induction system of Saleen's own design, the SSC could pump out 275hp.

Moreover, the Saleen SSC had the look of a commemorative Mustang, with fully-functional ground-effects package, distinctive black, gray and yellow graphics, and purpose designed 16in DP wheels. The same could be said of the interior. All 292 SSCs featured a full

Left One of Saleen's advertising lines was: **"When you get serious about performance."** Team Saleen certainly was: this was one of the Mustangs they used to annex a second consecutive SCCA Escort Endurance Series championship in 1987.

Left and far left "For people who want more out of life than a little peace and quiet." While the Mustang GT certainly met that need, Steve Saleen and his Mustangs really rocked 'n' rolled! In this 1989 photo, taken for *Mustang Illustrated*, Steve proudly poses with a Saleen Mustang coupe, convertible, three-door and the SSC.

75

rollcage, Pioneer stereo, special 25th-anniversary serial-numbered badging, and Flofit seats covered in luxurious yellow, black and white leather. Without doubt, the Saleen SSC was a fitting tribute to 25 years' production of America's favorite ponycar.

What was to come?

Speculation was running high as to what the next generation of Mustang might look like as the current form entered its eleventh year of production in 1990. Ford appeased those fans who had been disappointed by its lackluster observance of the car's 25th anniversary by introducing the limited-edition Anniversary Green (sheesh!) 5.0-liter Mustang LX convertible, which was available with optional clearcoat paint.

That year the company also incorporated the federally mandated driver's air bag supplementary restraint system into the Mustang, deleting the ever popular tilt steering column in the process. For whatever reason, the remote cable operated gas-filler door was also no longer fitted. Go figure!

Over in the Saleen camp, the SC, (an improved version of the SSC) was stealing all the thunder. Unlike the SSC, how-

Above **Although Ford did little to celebrate the 25th anniversary of the Mustang, fans of the ponycar could attend the "Fabulous Fords Forever" celebration at Knott's Berry Farm, Buena Park, California. This poster advertised the event.**

Right **"It's a great way to enjoy the weekend... every day of the week", Ford reckoned in this 1990 advertisement for the LX ragtop.**

MUSTANG CHRONOLOGY – 1989

● As an underwhelming tribute to the Mustang's 25th anniversary, Ford installs a running-horse badge on the dash of all Mustangs built between April 17, 1989 and April 17, 1990.

● Specialty car converters Steeda Autosport (Pompano Beach, Florida), DECH Mustang, (Concord, Ontario, Canada) and Kenny Brown/Project Industries (Omaha, Nebraska) enter the late-model Mustang aftermarket.

● The Saleen SSC debuts to rave reviews. Distinctive looks, uprated engine and suspension, and eye catching graphics set this pony apart from the remainder of the herd.

● Swiss based Englishman John

Manners organizes the American Pony Drive. After shipping their ponycars to Jacksonville, Florida, a contingent of European Mustang enthusiasts begins a cross-country trek to the 25th-anniversary celebration at Knott's Berry Farm, Buena Park, California. Stopping at pre-arranged locations along the way, Manners' group arrives in Southern California a little worse for wear, but nonetheless on time.

● Steve Saleen cuts his teeth in the SCCA Trans-Am class, driving his General Tire backed Mustang.

● For the second year in a row, Jack Roush's Whistler sponsored IMSA GTO Mustangs dominate the Daytona 24-hour endurance classic.

ever, the SC could be ordered in more than one color.

Twin plugs

Content with the 5.0-liter's role as the mainstay powerplant for the Mustang, Ford directed its engineering energies toward the 2.3-liter OHC four. New for 1991 would be a twin-spark-plug cylinder head and dual ignition. This setup would increase the power of the anemic four-banger from 86 to 105hp.

Over in the V-8 camp, both Mustang LX and GT were treated to a wheel and tire upgrade, comprising 16x7in five-spoke alloy wheels wrapped with Michelin P225/55ZR XGT radial rubber. Also new that year was a redesigned convertible top stack, which allowed the top to sit 1½in lower in its well when it was folded down.

Once again, Saleen didn't leave Mustang fans disappointed with its newly introduced Vortech supercharger package, which boosted the power rating to 325hp. Old Steve also offered some new 17in wheels, shod with BF Goodrich Comp T/A rubber,

This page **The spread ad commemorates Team Roush's phenomenal domination of IMSA's GTO class with eight consecutive victories at the 24-hour Daytona endurance event. Also shown is one of the two cars run by the team in the 1990 event.**

as well as a Spyder option package for the convertible.

Maintaining interest

With rumors of the all-new 1994 ponycar running rampant, Ford attempted to maintain the level of interest in the 1992 model by offering the Special Edition Mustang LX convertible. This was painted Vibrant Red, which was offset by a white leather interior and top, and a set of pearl white, 16in, star-pattern wheels.

The Saleen Mustang would also be challenged by a factory group known as the Special Vehicle Team, who developed the SVT Mustang Cobra. Although referred to as a 1993 model, the SVT Cobra appeared in mid-1992. It could be considered a true factory hot rod, having a GT-40 equipped, 235hp engine and Borg-Warner T-5 five-speed manual transmission.

The SVT Cobra's suspension system featured a 28.5mm front anti-sway bar, stiffer front and rear springs, 10.84in front and 10.07in rear vented disc brakes, and Koni shock absorbers. Special 17in seven-spoke wheels were shod with Goodyear Eagle P245/45ZR radial rubber.

The SVT Mustang Cobra featured slightly restyled body panels, which could have come from either Mustang LX or GT. The interior was detailed with a white-faced, 160mph speedometer and accompanying instrumentation, along with either Ebony or Opal Gray leather trim. SVT also took much of the difficulty out of deciding which exterior color to order by offering three basic

---

MUSTANG CHRONOLOGY – 1991

● Twin-plug head and distributor-less electronic ignition are incorporated on the OHC four.

● New 16in alloy wheels and Michelin XGT radial tires are offered on the LX and GT.

● Saleen introduces the SC package.

● Roush Racing does it again at the Daytona 24-hour classic.

● Seriously encroaching upon Saleen territory, the SAAC Car Company, a division of the Shelby American Automobile Club, debuts the 330hp SAAC MK-I three-door, and later the MK-II convertible.

These pages **The phrase, "Now you're cookin' with gas", was borrowed from 1950s Southern California Gas Company commercials. Also shown are a 1992 Limited Edition Mustang LX** (*left*) **and a 1992 Saleen Mustang** (*facing page*).

GO AHEAD,
MAKE YOUR DAY.

I DARE U

FORD MUSTANG GT

HAVE YOU DRIVEN
A FORD LATELY?

choices: Vibrant Red, Ebony and Teal clearcoat metallic.

Still a winner

With the end of an illustrious 14-year production run in sight, the 1993 Mustang was anything but mundane. Two Limited Edition 5.0-liter Mustang LX convertibles were prepared for the cruising crowd. They sported a choice of black or white leather interiors (personalized with "pony" floor mats); black or white soft top; chrome or white, 16in, star-pattern wheels; and yellow or white paintwork.

High performance freaks could rejoice in the introduction of the SVT Mustang Cobra R-model, built specifically for racing. Basically, this car was a stripped version of the regular SVT Mustang Cobra, and all 107 vehicles were spoken for months before they were actually constructed.

In preparation for 1994 Mustang production, Ford incorporated the low-profile induction-system equipped, 205hp, 5.0-liter V-8 into the 1993 line.

Steve Saleen seized the opportunity of celebrating both the last of the Fox Mustangs and his company's tenth anniversary by releasing ten black 10th Anniversary Saleen Mustangs. Complete with striking yellow and white graphics, these cars were sold by advance registration, and they sold quickly. Like the SSC and SC, they had certain unique features, such as vented composite hoods, four-wheel disc brakes, Saleen Racecraft panhard rod and rear shock tower brace, white-faced Saleen instrumentation, full rollcage and Recaro seats.

MUSTANG CHRONOLOGY – 1992-93

● The Special Edition Mustang LX convertible is introduced in 1992, as is the SVT Mustang Cobra, which challenges the Saleen Mustang.

● Limited Edition Mustang LX convertibles are introduced in 1993.

● SCCA Escort Endurance Series

racer Chris Kaufmann captures his first series title in 1993, driving a race prepared Mustang LX.

● The SVT Mustang Cobra R-model sells out prior to production.

● Team Roush wins the Daytona 24-hour race again!

● 1993 sees the debut of the limited-edition 10th Anniversary Saleen Mustang. Saleen also builds a special one-off Mustang for Tim Allen, star of the television sitcom *Home Improvement*. Sporting special bodywork and powered by a 650hp 5.0-liter V-8, "Tim's Toy" is a genuine 200mph street car.

Facing page, top right
With 1993 being the Fox Mustang's last hurrah, Ford and JWT attempted to deplete new car inventories by modifying a memorable Clint Eastwood line, used in the film *Dirty Harry*. It simply stated: "Go ahead, make your day."

Facing page, top left
Steve Saleen's last shot at marketing his Fox based model continued the theme: "When you get serious about performance."

Facing page, bottom
Artist's renderings of Saleen's very limited-edition 10th Anniversary Mustang.

Left **The 1993 SVT Mustang Cobra.**

IT IS WHAT IT WAS
AND MORE

THE ALL-NEW
MUSTANG

MOTOR TREND
CAR OF THE YEAR

It was the car that captured a generation.

It was performance designed for flying by the seat of your pants.

It was vinyl bucket seats and standard lap belts.

It was the car that made automotive history.

It is that same spirit captured in an all-new shape.

It is a new generation of performance, harnessed by a tuned suspension.

It is an ergonomically designed cockpit and standard dual air bags.

It is Motor Trend's 1994 Car of the Year. It is the all-new Ford Mustang.

HAVE YOU DRIVEN
A FORD LATELY?

Ford

Always wear your safety belts with your driver and right front passenger supplemental restraint system.

Right **To generate interest in the 1994 Mustang, Ford traded heavily on nostalgia and brand loyalty, using ads such as this.**

82

CHAPTER 7

A New Era: 1994-96

After much anticipation, and a few well placed publicity leaks to sustain the American public's interest, the 1994 Ford Mustang, (project code SN-95) made its first official appearance on the morning of October 9, 1993, at the State Fair of Texas in Fair Park, Dallas. Presiding over the festivities was vice president of Ford Division Ross Roberts who, with the assistance of two cheerleaders from the Dallas Cowboys football team, unveiled a Laser Red GT convertible in front of delegates from the Texas Auto Writer's Association.

In typical western fashion, an identical ragtop was presented at "high noon" to a crowd of over 30,000 in front of the new car product building on the State Fair of Texas Midway. Ford public affairs manager Mike Moran and Dallas PR zone office chief Jim Bright cleverly concealed the GT in a huge wooden crate. On the front of the crate was a large shipping label that read: "TO: FORD MOTOR COMPANY, TEXAS STATE FAIR, DALLAS, TEXAS 75315." A return address read: "FORD MOTOR COMPANY, DEARBORN ASSEMBLY PLANT, DETROIT, MI. 48121."

Heightening the suspense was a digital clock, counting down the seconds. At the stroke of twelve, a "passel" of red, white and blue balloons was released into the sky, the sides of the box dropped away, and the rest, as they say, is (Mustang) history!

The following weekend, October 17-18, Ford staged a cleverly devised 100-city media blitz, working in conjunction with Mustang and Shelby enthusiast clubs, such as the Mustang Club of America, Shelby American Automobile Club, Late Model Mustang Owners' Association and the SVO Owners' Association. Ford dispatched a key executive to each city, with both Mustang V-6 and GT models being previewed initially.

Left **The Dearborn Styling Studio's "Schwarzenegger" full-size clay is shown alongside an example of its predecessor during an October, 1990 review of the SN-95 Mustang development program.**

Right **A fully finished Confirmation Prototype (CP) clay produced some time in 1992.**

Below **Members of the automotive media were allowed to drive post-production versions of the 1994 Mustang in July, 1993 at the Dearborn Proving Grounds. Here, Team Mustang's O.J. Coletti explains the finer points of a 3.8-liter V-6 convertible to one of the journalists while travelling at speed.**

Some of the more notable launch locations included:

Mustang, Oklahoma, at the intersection of Oklahoma state highway 152 and Mustang Road.

The Goodyear blimp base, Carson, California.

Alexandria, Virginia, at Potomac River Park. Ford CEO Harold "Red" Poling presided.

The former New York World's Fair Hemisphere site at Flushing Meadows. A 300-car classic Mustang celebration also took place at the same time.

The Hard Rock Cafe, Universal Studios, Orlando, Florida.

The *USS Lexington* aircraft carrier, Corpus Christi, Texas.

The historic Chicago White Sox baseball park, Soldier Field, Chicago, Illinois.

The Alamo, San Antonio, Texas.

In all, over 7000 classic and late-model Mustangs (and their owners) would attend these launches. Furthermore, well over 150,000 spectators would flock to view the new Mustang, while 110 major newspapers and 45 television stations would cover these events. There was much more to come. But what about the sensational new machines themselves?

Placed in charge of the SN-95 program was former Ford engineering and operations manager Will Boddie. The chief program manager was O.J. "John" Coletti, former leader of the "Skunkworks" team, the group responsible for the all-important engineering and design feasibility study on the Mustang. Appointed SN-95 business planning manager was Ron Muccioli, while John Aken and Bud Magaldi filled the positions of design executive and design manager. Mike Ferrence would be named marketing plans manager, while Dia Hothi and Ron Pollard were given the positions of manufacturing and finance managers respectively. These were the key figures in Team Mustang.

One of the main requirements set down by management was that the car should be contemporary, yet affordable. This was in line with Ford's overall 30% cost reduction/new car development program mandate, which had to be stringently adhered to. As a result, the 16-year-old Fox unibody platform (previously used on the Fairmont, as well as the Mustang) was chosen as a base. Although somewhat dated, this platform proved a solid starting point. Placed in charge of the chassis design program was Ken Christensen.

With the new Mustang being 0.8in longer than its predecessor, and wider overall by 3.7in, good ride and handling were key chassis engineering objectives. Moving the #2 front crossmember 17.8mm further forward not only stretched the Mustang's wheelbase to 101.3in, but also allowed for the proposed installation of the considerably larger, 4.6-liter, modular DOHC powerplant in the 1996 model. This modification also afforded chassis engineers the opportunity of revising the Fox's front suspension geometry, providing cam-

ber/castor settings of ±1.5-4.0 degrees. Slightly longer gas charged Monroe front struts and longer lower control arms were also incorporated, along with a 30mm (27mm on the V-6 car) tubular anti-sway bar. Variable-ratio, power assisted rack-and-pinion steering was standard on both models.

Back again was the previous Mustang's rear suspension, utilizing unequal-length upper and lower control arms, progressive-rate coil springs and a Monroe Quadra-Shock setup. The 8.8in live axle was available with gear ratios ranging from 2.73:1 to 3.27:1. A 24mm tubular rear anti-sway bar was standard on the GT, while a slightly smaller 21mm bar was used on the V-6.

The new Mustang sported power-assisted, four-wheel disc brakes (10.8in front and 10.5in rear) on both the GT and V-6. A Bosch ABS2U anti-lock package was also available as an option on both models.

Rolling stock comprised 6.5x15in steel safety rims with Goodyear P205/65R GA

Below **Ford Division and JWT commissioned this aerial billboard to fly over San Diego's convention center during the Ford dealer's convention in August 1993.**

Right and below right **On October 9, 1993, in front of a large crowd of eager Texans, Ross Roberts, vice president of Ford Division, was assisted by two comely Dallas Cowboys cheerleaders in the first public unveiling of a Laser Red 1994 Mustang GT convertible at the State Fair of Texas. The large packing crate was employed in the outdoor unveiling of an identical model.**

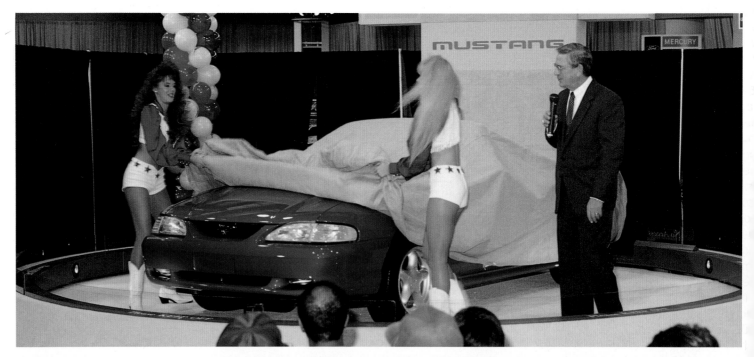

ls, a simulated mag-design hubcap
g fitted to the baseline V-6.
ermore, an optional 7.9x15in,
-spoke, cast-aluminum wheel was
able. When it came to the GT,
6in, five-spoke alloy wheels,
ped with Firestone P225/55ZR All-
ons, were standard. An 8.0x17in,
-spoke alloy wheel, shod with
dyear Eagle GT 245/45ZR rubber,
the top option.

ally, two powerplants would moti-
the new ponycars. Underneath the
py hood of the GT was the trusty
ter V-8, which was rated at 215hp.
engine was equipped with 9.0:1-
pression, silicone-alloy pistons; a
-cam valvetrain; low-profile, EEC-V
aged SEFI with 19lb/hr Bosch fuel
tors and 65mm throttle body; and
ar exhaust headers.

e Mustang's 3.8-liter V-6 was also a
y little package. It featured a 9.0:1
pression ratio, swirl-chamber alu-
m heads and SEFI. It was capable
mping out 145hp at 4000rpm.

o returning as the gearbox of
ce on the 1994 model was the Borg-
er T-5. Ford's electronically man-
l AOD-E four-speed automatic
mission was offered for the "stab it,
steer it" crowd.

cording to Team Mustang design
r Bud Magaldi, the primary objec-
f the team's stylists was to design a
at had contemporary aerodynamic
g, yet emulated the all-important
ang look. Taking various styling
from past models, the team devel-
a shape that featured an updated
on of the classic Mustang air intake,
lete with traditional running-horse
em. Flanking this was a pair of low-

THE LEGEND CONTINUES

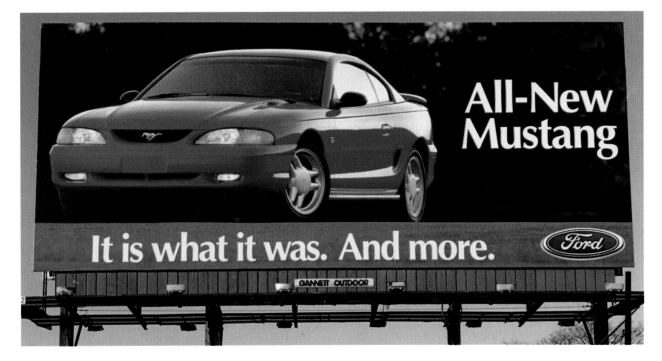

All-New
Mustang

It is what it was. And more.

Right **Dealer promo model cars have always played an important role in the marketing of any new Ford. The 1994 Mustang was no exception, and ERTL duly offered this pair of red and yellow 1/25-scale coupes, which were made in China.**

Below **Important news for 1994 was the release of the limited-edition SVT Mustang Cobra Indianapolis 500 Pace Car convertible. This commemorated the Mustang's third go-round as the official pace car for the "Greatest Spectacle In Motor Racing".**

profile, wrap-around, flush-fit, halogen headlamps accompanied by amber turn signals and parking lamps. The new model's pliable urethane nosecap also featured a sculpted spoiler, with central air intake, and "cat's eye" running lights. The ribbed hood incorporated a bold scoop, while the indented flanks were reminiscent of past Mustangs.

The roofline was swept back and afforded the occupants maximum visibility, while the stubby rear end featured a small aerodynamic kick up on the decklid. Horizontally-slatted taillamps and a pliable rear bumpercap, with dual exhaust tips below it, were all part of this aesthetically pleasing package. Initially, the car was offered in a choice of 11 eye popping clearcoat colors.

Ergonomics played a major role in the interior design of the car. Its twin-pod, soft-touch dash faintly echoed the early Mercedes and Corvette. Contained within its instrument cluster was a 150mph speedometer and 7000rpm tachometer. Back again was tilt steering with soft-touch, leather wrapped steering wheel. The sculpted door panels concealed a pair of safety-beam door guards. The GT's Lear Seating Corporation, leather-wrapped, CAD designed, four-way power adjusted bucket seats provided optimum support and comfort. New that year was a CFC-free air conditioning system and an optional Mach 460 stereo system, which was capable of blowing the windows out of the car parked next to you! It was that good.

Although the Mustang was available in only two models initially, an SVT Mustang Cobra Indianapolis 500 Pace Car convertible was waiting in the wings. For the third time in Mustang history, America's favorite ponycar would be pacing the Memorial Day classic. All 1000 of the 1994 Indy Pace Car Cobras featured 235hp 5.0-liter engines, T-5 five-speed manual transmissions, 3.27:1 rear-end gearing, uprated suspension, and distinctive cast-aluminum, vented 17in wheels, wrapped in Goodyear GSC P225/ZR45 radial rubber.

Up front, the nosecap featured sculpted openings on each side of its air dam with tunneled quartz halogen driving lights. The standard Mustang headlamps were replaced by high-intensity, clear-lens halogen units.

Inside, special Pace Car badging, tan leather seats and a street version of the genuine pace car's light bar (minus the

strobe light and emergency flasher) was incorporated. The Pace Car came in just one color, Rio Red, with tastefully executed "Official Pace Car" graphics. This was one heck of a beautiful machine.

Steady improvement

In terms of Mustang production, 1995 paled in comparison to the previous calendar year. Nonetheless, the Mustang was not resting on its laurels. Quietly

Left **Bird Corporation's Indy Pace Car replicas featured 3.5hp Briggs gasoline engines, which were capable of propelling the little chargers to speeds of 20mph. A 5hp Briggs engine was available as a go-faster option.**

Below **This assortment of goodies includes an official Pace Car jacket, a Pace Car pin (on the lapel), a Pace Car key fob (attached to the zipper), a 1/18-scale limited-edition die-cast model by Jouef, and a Pace Car poster. All were available through SVT dealers.**

MUSTANG CHRONOLOGY — 1994

● August 1989. Ford CEO, Harold "Red" Poling assigns the task of assembling a team, to develop a new Mustang, to NAAO executive vice president Alex Trotman. He passes the baton to small car programs manager Ken Dabrowski, who brings in small car engineering design manager O.J. Coletti. In turn, he picks a group of enthusiastic Ford talent.

● February 1990. The first clay mock-up is shown to Alex Trotman. The Ford VP likes what he sees and encourages further development.

● June 1990. Two finished clays are prepared: the Hutting Design Center's "California" design and the Dearborn generated "Bruce Jenner" offering.

● October 1990. Two more clays are produced. The "Rambo" configuration is considered too aggressive, while the "Arnold Schwarzenegger" version appears to be closest to the actual production vehicle of 1994. This ultimately receives the go-ahead.

● August 1991. The first structural prototype (SP) is finished, followed by the confirmed prototype (CP) in October.

● November 1991. Members of the automotive enthusiast magazine industry are shown the new model.

● November 1992. The first Mustang Mach III show car is completed by Masco-Tech Industries of Hammtramack, Michigan.

● March 1993. The first pilot production 1994 Mustangs are built at the Dearborn Assembly Plant.

● July 1993. The automotive media test drive the new Mustang at the long-lead press program, held at the Dearborn Proving Grounds. The ponycar receives rave reviews.

● August 1993. The 1994 Mustangs are the center of attention at the annual Ford Dealers' Convention in San Diego, California.

● August 1993. Steve Saleen begins his latest Mustang design: the S-351.

● September 1993. Ford stages its 1994 Mustang short-lead press preview at the Alisal Guest Ranch, Solvang, California. Journalists are treated to a 300+ mile drive through the backroads of Owens Valley.

● October 4, 1993. The first new Mustang is driven off the Dearborn assembly line by outgoing CEO Poling and incoming CEO Trotman.

● October 9, 1993. Ross Roberts officiates at the Mustang's first public unveiling at the State Fair of Texas.

● October 17, 1993. Ford conducts a 100-city media blitz.

● November 20, 1993. The country's top 100 Ford dealers are given their chance to drive the new ponycar for the first time at the Palm Springs, California "Mustang Fantasy Camp".

● November 1993. Ford and JWT run TV spots over Thanksgiving weekend.

● December 8, 1993. *Motor Trend* magazine awards the new Mustang its prestigious Car of the Year award.

● December 9, 1993. The official introduction day for the new car.

● December 10, 1993. Ford and JWT place a multi-fold poster in *USA Today*. The newspaper is a sell-out.

● Ford racers Jack Roush and Bob Glidden complete their respective SCCA Trans-Am and NHRA Pro-Stock race cars in time for the celebrations.

● January 1994. NHRA and IMSA racer Paul Rossi fields a four-car Clean-Air Cobra team.

● Roush team driver Tommy Kendall annexes the 1994 SCCA Trans-Am championship.

UNBRIDLED ENTHUSIASM

THE ALL-NEW MUSTANG

"The latest and best Mustang hits the ground running."
Road & Track

"The new Mustang is solid, quiet, stable and thoroughly locked to the road."
Popular Mechanics

"Road feel is excellent, handling is superb."
The Chicago Tribune

"The all-new interior is nothing short of a design triumph."
AutoWeek

"Mustang handles more sure footedly than ever before."
Car & Driver

"Its first class styling, dynamics, and performance make it the most significant new American car this year."
Motor Trend

HAVE YOU DRIVEN A FORD LATELY?

Always wear your safety belt.

Above **This Mustang Pace Car belt buckle was one of several Ford promotional items offered during 1994.**

Above left **This JWT advertisement for the GT has a catchy line in phrases: "It Kicks And Screams Just Like The Day It Was Born."**

Left **While this particular advertisement touts the features of the entry-level Mustang V-6, Steve Saleen had other plans for this car. He created the notorious S-351 Mustang, using the V-6 as a starting point. Since quite a few modifications had to be made to the car, including yanking out the complete powertrain, he figured that he might as well start off with the cheap model.**

91

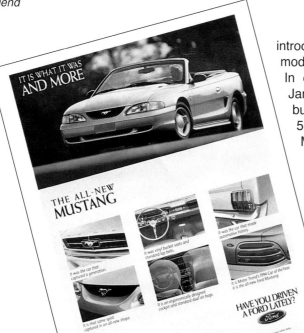

introduced that year was a no-frills V-8 model, known as the Mustang GTS. In essence, this shared the plain-Jane coachwork of the Mustang V-6, but it was powered by the 215hp 5.0-liter V-8 normally found in the Mustang GT.

The SVT Mustang Cobra, however, was an entirely different story. Basically, the limited-production SVT Cobra was virtually identical in appearance to 1994's Indy 500 Pace Car, but with a hardtop and without the decal graphics. Unlike the Pace Car, the SVT

Mustang Cobra was offered in a choice of three colours: Rio Red, Crystal White and Black.

Also released that year was a very limited-edition SVT Mustang Cobra, which sported a removable hardtop. Due to myriad production problems with subcontractors, this particular model was cancelled and the vehicles were quietly sold off through participating SVT dealers. Very little was said publicly.

Conversely, a great deal was said about the Dearborn built SVT Mustang Cobra R-model. Developed primarily for competition, this no-nonsense Mustang was outfitted with racing suspension; a

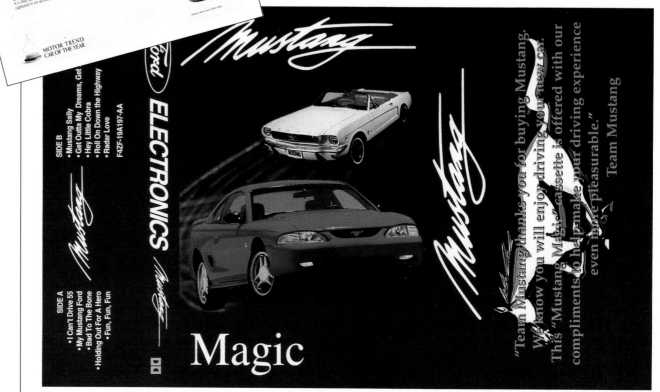

330hp, GT-40 equipped 351-W Lightning Truck engine package; heavy-duty radiator, oil and transmission coolers; a Tremec 3550 five-speed transmission; uprated Cobra four-wheel disc brakes (13.0in front and 11.85in rear); 17in five-spoke R-model "artillery" wheels, shod with specially formulated BF Goodrich P255/45ZR Comp T/A radial rubber; a 20-gallon fuel cell; a racing hood; "strippo" interior; and Crystal White clearcoat paint. In total, Ford built 200 of these factory hot rods, and they all found buyers quite quickly.

On the aftermarket front, few would argue that Steve Saleen's latest genera-

This page **Given that an entirely new car had been launched in the 30th-anniversary year of the Mustang, it was not considered necessary to produce a specific commemorative model. However, Ford and JWT did create an official 30th-anniversary Mustang logo, along with a series of promotional items. Among these were a reflection poster (depicting both 1964½ and 1994 Mustangs), golf shirts, hats, coffee mugs and decals.**

Right **On the heels of the Indy 500 Pace Car came the 1995 release of the SVT Mustang Cobra. This vehicle was identical in specification to its open-air counterpart, with the exception of the Pace Car commemorative items.**

tion of specialty Mustangs aren't about the best looking cars to be seen on the road. Even fewer would suggest that a Saleen S-351 isn't one of the fastest cars on the road!

A controversial change

When it comes to the recently introduced, 4.6-liter "mod-motored" Mustangs of 1996, it's been our experience that you either love them or hate them. The installation of Ford's two-valve and four-valve modular V-8 powerplants in the 1996 Mustang GT and SVT Cobra

Right **The SVT Mustang Cobra was available with a removable hardtop option, but only 586 were released before production problems forced Ford to abandon the project. Shown here is the rarest removable-hardtop SVT Mustang Cobra of all,** *Mustang Illustrated* **magazine's Saleen S-351, which was given away as the prize in a subscription drive.**

appears to have caused quite a rift among Mustang fans.

On one side, there are the pushrod V-8 traditionalists, who argue that the 215hp, SOHC, 4.6-liter, two-valve mod motor in the GT, and the 305hp, four-valve, DOHC V-8 in the SVT Cobra are too expensive, too sophisticated, too difficult to maintain and too slow. On the other, there are foresighted folks, who claim that the mod-motored Mustangs are the cars that Ford should have released in the first place, when they launched the 1994 model. Time, of course, will tell.

Left **Steve Saleen's Mystic painted, BASF sponsored S-351 giveaway convertible.**

Left **In 1995, Steve Saleen and** *Home Improvement* **star Tim Allen joined forces to form the Saleen/Allen RRR Speedlab Racing Team. Their target was the SCCA World Challenge title.**

After 108 Wins, 11 New Speed Records and 39 Pole Positions, We Can Hold Our Heads Up High.

{Along with a few things considerably heavier.}

If you think our 1995 racing totals or our trophies are impressive, just wait. Because if you really want to be impressed by a season in which we won 16 racing championships, consider this. Every time we take another checkered flag, we use our race-winning technology as inspiration for the Ford you can drive. Now there's a concept that carries some weight. WE RACE. YOU WIN.

Ford

These pages **A completely new generation of high-tech ponycars was ushered in with the 1994 debut of the "mod-motored", 4.6-liter, two-valve Mustang GT and four-valve SVT Cobra. The ad clearly conveys a message: Mustang high performance!**

MUSTANG CHRONOLOGY – 1995

● The no-frills Mustang GTS quietly debuts without a fanfare.

● Ford's Special Vehicle Team introduces the SVT Mustang Cobra and the low-volume, race-only R-model.

● Steeda Autosport's Dario Orlando and partner Dan Perkins' Strictly Biz Racing Mustang Cobra establishes itself as the fastest R-model in the country, winning the very first IMSA Grand Sport event for Ford in the process.

● Due to production problems, 586 SVT Mustang Cobras with removable hardtops are quietly sold off.

● Steve Saleen and *Mustang Illustrated* magazine transform an SVT Mustang Cobra with removable hardtop into probably the rarest of all Saleen Mustangs: the only S-351 with that option. This fabulous machine is offered as the prize in the magazine's year-long subscription drive.

● Steeda Autosport builds the Steeda Q-car, an affordable alternative to the expensive SVT Cobra R-model.

Right Plastic model kits and radio-controlled toys have been popular with Mustang enthusiasts since Day One. Shown are: Revell's *Hot Rod* magazine Monroe Handler Cobra II street racer in 1/25 scale; Model Products Corporation (MPC) three-door, 20th-anniversary 1984 Mustang GT-350 in 1/25 scale; Monogram's 1992 Mustang GT convertible and SN-95 Mustang, both in 1/25 scale; Maisto 1/18-scale, die-cast "Collector's Edition" 1970 Boss 302 Mustang; Revell's SnapTite 1/25-scale 1995 Shinoda Boss Mustang, personally autographed by Larry Shinoda, famed designer of the Boss 302 and Boss 429; JRL R/C Racing Mach III Mustang show car; Revell's die-cast 1/18-scale 30th-anniversary 1965 Mustang convertible; Monogram's 1/24-scale 1985 Mustang SVO; Tamiya's 1994 SN-95 Mustang; Maisto's 1/24-scale 1994 Mustang GT convertible.

CHAPTER 8

ALL THOSE WONDERFUL TOYS, AND THEN SOME!

ew automobiles manufactured during the past century have achieved the almost cult-like following of the Ford Mustang. As a result, the car has become a money-spinner among toy, clothing and novelty makers around the world. Whether it has the classic early

shape of the mid-1964 model or the high-tech, aerodynamic styling of today's wonder, the Ford Mustang is an all-time favorite with ponycar enthusiasts of all ages.

Assembled here are many examples of Mustang novelties, in the form of toys,

radio controlled cars, plastic model kits, games, playing and collector cards and, yes, even bottled after-shave lotion and cookies! Furthermore, what you see on these pages is only a small selection of the Mustang inspired items that are available world-wide.

Left **Little is known about the history of these Mustang Round-Up Rally badges from 1965 and 1966, although the badges themselves can often be found.**

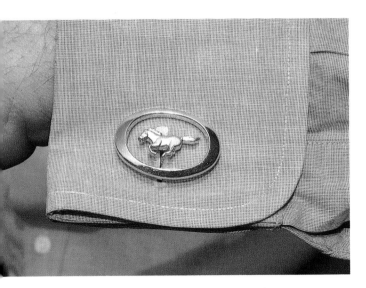

Left In the mid-1960s, Lesney (Matchbox Series) and Mattel (Hot Wheels) produced collector's carrying cases for their toy cars. Both bore illustrations of Mustangs: the Matchbox 1966 model and the Hot Wheels 1969-70 version.

Far left These Mustang cufflinks were specially made by a jeweler for retired Ford dealer John Mendel, Sr.

Facing page Among the promotional items that Ford dealers handed out in 1968 were these "Better Idea" playing cards. Vehicle descriptions and engineering data were printed on the playing side of each card.

Left In the 1970s, Avon produced a series of colored glass collector bottles filled with the company's best men's cologne. This 1966 Mustang bottle was one of two Ford products replicated by the well-known cosmetics and toiletries giant. The other was the 1956 Thunderbird.

101

Right **This 1966 Mustang desk lamp is of unknown origin, although it appears to be of Japanese manufacture. Pristine examples of this lamp are well worth adding to any collection of Mustang memorabilia.**

This page **These rare 1971-73 Mustang model kits were located at a flea market. The Jo-Han 1/25-scale Boss Hoss "Digger" Funny Car kit is a loose interpretation of famed speed king Mickey Thompson's 1971 AA/FC. The 1/32-scale 1973 Monogram Luminators model doesn't particularly resemble anyone's Mach 1 funny car from that era.**

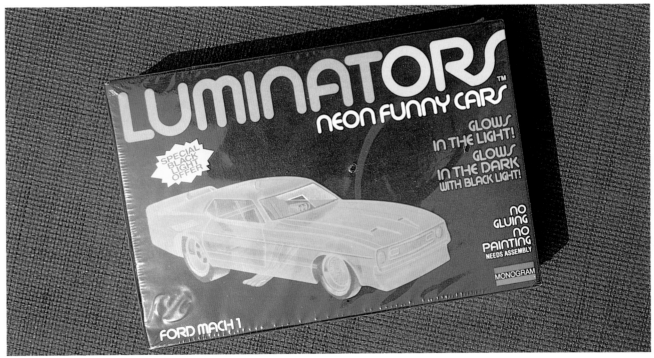

Right **Most people will have heard of animal crackers, but how about car cookies? Mustang car cookies are a product of fortune cookie maker Summerfield Foods. Inside each box are examples of the Mustang Mach III, 1965 Shelby GT-350, 1965 Mustang convertible, 1967 Shelby GT-500 and 1994 Mustang, in addition to four Ford Thunderbird models. Only in America!**

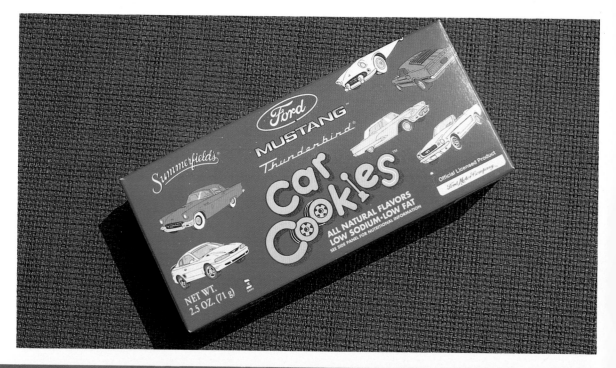

Right **In 1966, a French artisan took a 1966 Mustang fastback and rebodied it to reflect a more European style. That car went on to be known as the *Automobile Quarterly* Mustang. Today, its whereabouts are unknown, but this Japanese model of the car remains and is owned by Canadian Kelly McAndrew.**

Left **This trio of die-cast metal miniatures reflects the ongoing popularity of the early Mustang. From left to right: Mattel's Hot Wheels 1965 Mustang convertible, Johnny Lightning's Muscle Cars USA 1970 Boss 302 Mustang, and Jet Wheels' Chinese made 1965 Mustang coupe.**

Left **These two plaster Shelby Mustangs, from ponycar aficionado Don Chambers' collection, are of unknown origin. Most probably they were created by a classic Mustang enthusiast with a talent for sculpting.**

105

Left Pogs were an American collector fad of the mid-1990s. Sets like this What's Next? Productions pack of ten licensed Mustang 30th Anniversary Collector's Series pogs were the hot ticket, if only briefly.

Far left In the mid-1990s, Galoob Toys unveiled its meticulously detailed Micro Machines toy line. Shown here is the company's Mustang collection.

Facing page This group of Mustang collectibles could easily fit into your coat pocket, and it would be a fairly valuable "stash" to say the least. Included are a pair of Mattel Hot Wheels Mustang fastbacks; a Mustang running-horse chocolate, circa 1993; Special Vehicle Team stick pin; two different Mustang 30th-anniversary pins; Mustang cufflink and tie clip; 25th-anniversary Mustang dash emblem; AmeriVox Mustang 30th-anniversary phone card; 30th-anniversary Mustang pin assortment and belt buckle; Shell Oil "Shellzone" 1/64-scale die-cast Roush Racing Trans-Am Mustang; and examples of an Avon pewter key chain and Hallmark poly-covered Mustang key chain.

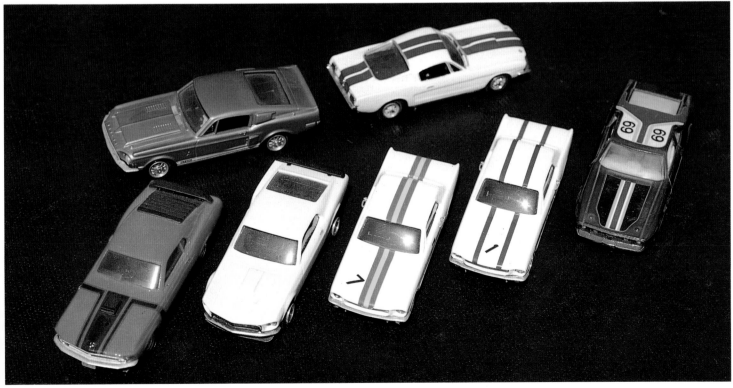

Left These 1/64-scale Shelbys and Mustangs are of Australian, US and French manufacture.

Right The battle of the booze bottles continued in the mid-1990s with the release of Jim Beam's serial-numbered, 1965 Mustang decanters. Available in red, white or black, and sporting a removable plastic top, these decanters contained a full quart of the company's finest Kentucky straight bourbon whiskey.

Right Recently introduced is a reproduction of the ever popular AMF stamped-steel Midget Mustang of 1964. These replicas are available in a number of colors, as well as in 1964 Indianapolis 500 Pace Car guise, from companies such as Tony D. Branda Shelby & Mustang Parts (Altoona, Pa.) and Dallas Mustang Parts (Dallas, Texas). While the originals retailed for $12⁹⁵, however, these reproductions have a price tag close to $400⁰⁰!

This page **The famous blue-striped, white Shelby GT-350 Mustang of 1965 has been replicated in die-cast form by both European toy manufacturer Joef (GT-350 street version) and domestic model manufacturer Revell (R-model race version), in 1/18-scale and 1/25-scale respectively.**

SALES AND PRODUCTION FIGURES (US MODEL)

Model year	Hardtop	Convertible	Fastback/3-door	Total sales	Model year production
1964½	91,532	28,468	0	120,000	121,538
1965	365,215,	65,244	68,784	499,243	559,451
1966	450,352	64,990	32,169	547,511	607,568
1967	334,059	42,014	66,613	442,686	472,121
1968	235,031	23,910	40,120	299,061	317,404
1969	147,381	14,427	131,530	293,338	299,824
1970	85,703	6,839	77,461	170,003	190,727
1971	77,697	5,723	56,523	139,943	149,678
1972	72,277	6,136	41,507	119,920	125,093
1973	70,229	10,845	42,327	123,401	134,867
1974	204,892	0	91,149	296,041	385,993
1975	145,220	0	53,979	199,199	188,575
1976	110,440	0	68,101	178,541	187,567
1077	102,680	0	58,974	161,654	153,173
1978	107,971	0	71,068	179,039	192,410
1979	188,150	0	114,159	302,309	369,936
1980	123,435	0	122,573	246,008	271,322
1981	88,838	0	84,491	173,329	182,552
1982	46,159	0	70,645	116,804	130,418
1983	31,299	23,620	61,202	116,121	120,873
1984	35,092	16,950	79,719	131,761	141,480
1985	59,122	16,182	84,437	159,741	156,514
1986	67,456	19,550	88,592	175,598	224,410
1987	44,085	23,599	95,708	163,392	159,145
1988	38,291	26,838	105,472	170,601	211,225
1989	31,847	35,309	105,062	172,218	209,769
1990	18,611	26,708	75,168	120,487	128,189
1991	16,876	20,143	53,441	90,460	98,737
1992	13,428	22,235	36,241	71,904	79,096
1993	20,127	24,063	52,035	96,225	114,228
Total	3,423,495	523,793	2,129,250	6,076,538	6,683,883

ACKNOWLEDGMENTS

The authors would like to thank the following for their invaluable assistance in the preparation of this book:

Don and Ailene Chambers, MUSTANG COUNTRY, Paramount, California.
O.J. Coletti, Director, Special Vehicle Engineering, FORD MOTOR COMPANY, Dearborn, Michigan.
Austin C. Craig, Ford Account Executive, J.WALTER THOMPSON, INC, Detroit, Michigan.
John Clinard, Western Region Ford Public Affairs Director, FORD MOTOR COMPANY, Anaheim, California.
Barbara E. McClurg, North Hollywood, California.
Victor and Marjorie McClurg, Hillsdale, New York.

Bill Porter, President, McMULLEN ARGUS PUBLISHING COMPANY, Placentia, California.
John Mendel, Western Region Sales Manager, FORD MOTOR COMPANY, Dearborn, Michigan.
Bill Norton, VALLEY FORD PARTS COMPANY, North Hollywood, California.
Arnie, Jack and Patty Redeker, REDEKER FORD, Grand Haven, Michigan.
Steve and Liz Saleen, SALEEN PERFORMANCE, Irvine, California.
Jim and Sharon Slack, COPPERSTATE MUSTANG CLUB, Mesa, Arizona.
Lonnie Walter, CARS & STRIPES, Mesquite, Texas.
Doris and Sid Willsheer.

Andy Willsheer and Bob McClurg met in the 1970s when the former, an Englishman, was in Southern California, photographing the action at a National Hot Rod Association national drag racing event. McClurg was already a well established name among the drag racing photographic fraternity, while Willsheer was attempting to get a foot in the door, so to speak. Sharing, among other things, a devotion to the quarter-mile sport and, oddly, a warped sense of humor, the twosome hit it off and over the years have kept in touch, their paths usually crossing at the drag strip.

Although McClurg's automotive photo-journalistic talents were widely recognized and put to use in many US publications — *Super Stock*, *Hot Rod*, *Drag Racing*, *Kit Car* and, most recently, *Mustang Illustrated* and *Ford High Performance* (he is editor of both) — Willsheer has always regarded drag racing as his primary interest, other journalistic tasks taking second place.

However, with McClurg being an aficionado of the Ford Mustang (he and his wife own several), it was inevitable that Willsheer would broaden his remit to include the famous ponycar, and he is currently the European editor of McMullen Argus Publishing's *Mustang Illustrated* and *Ford High Performance*.

Aside from covering the major straight-line races in England, the Cheshunt, Hertfordshire resident generally manages to take in four NHRA national events each year. While McClurg's travels haven't yet taken him to the UK, he and wife Barbara have, for more than a decade, welcomed the traveling limey to their Toluca Lake, California home where the Anglo-American alliance ha collaborated on a variety of assign ments, including Windrow & Greene' *Classics in Colour: Ford Mustang*.

This is their second book on the sub ject of America's favorite ponycar, an they hope that readers will gain as muc enjoyment from the story of selling th Mustang legend as they did from compi ing the material.

Andy Willsheer

Bob McClurg